To

———————————————————————

From

———————————————————————

DOTUN
OYEWOPO

THE GLORIOUS WOMAN

DOTUN
OYEWOPO

THE GLORIOUS WOMAN

PUBLISHED IN AUSTRALIA BY
ACHIEVERS WORLD

The Glorious Woman

Copyright © 2019 by Dotun Oyewopo.

All rights reserved.

Requests for information should be addressed to:
dotunoyewopo@gmail.com

This book, or parts thereof, may not be reproduced, stored in a retrieval system, or transmitted in any form or by any means, electronic, mechanical, photocopying, recording or otherwise, without the written permission of the publisher.

ISBN 978-0-6482834-4-7 (paperback)
ISBN 978-0-6482834-8-5 (ebook)

Printed in Australia

Every attempt has been made to credit the sources of copyrighted material used in this book. If any such acknowledgment has been inadvertently omitted or miscredited, receipt of such information would be appreciated

Unless otherwise noted, all scriptures are from *The Holy Bible, New International Version.* Copyright © 1973, 1978, 1984, 2011 by Biblica, Inc.® Used by permission of Zondervan. All rights reserved worldwide. www.Zondervan.com.

Scripture quotations marked (KJV) are taken from the *King James Version of the Bible.*

Scripture quotations marked (NLT) are from the *Holy Bible, New Living Translation.* Copyright © 1996, 2004, 2007 by Tyndale House Foundation. Used by permission of Tyndale House Publishers Inc., Carol Stream, Illinois 60188. All rights reserved.

Scripture quotations marked (GW) are taken from GOD'S WORD® Copyright© 1995 by God's Word to the Nations. All rights reserved

Words and phrases in Scripture quotations that are in **bold** or *italics* are the emphasis of the author.

DEDICATION

This book is dedicated to all women. It is dedicated to you. This moment in your life is precious because God has destined that today, you will hold this book *The Glorious Woman* in your hands. It is God's will to make His glory shine through you and for you to discover who you are in Him.

Arise, shine, for your light has come, and the glory of the LORD rises upon you. See, darkness overs the earth and thick darkness is over the peoples, but the LORD rises upon you and his glory appears over you. Nations will come to your light, and kings to the brightness of your dawn. "Lift up your eyes and look about you: All assemble and come to you; your sons come from afar, and your daughters are carried on the hip. Then you will look and be radiant, your heart will throb and swell with joy; the wealth on the seas will be brought to you, to you the riches of the nations will come (Isaiah 60:1-5).

Acknowledgment

I acknowledge the Maker of heaven and the earth, the almighty God, the inspirational giver, the giver of visions and dreams. You are worthy of my praise. You gave me the book title, as well as wisdom and knowledge through the Holy Spirit. I couldn't have done it without you.

To my dearest husband, Oluwafemi Emmanuel Oyekunle Oyewopo, thank you for believing in me. You are my hero. You challenged me by setting the standard high. You gave me a push. Thank you for staying awake with me. I love you, my husband.

To my father-in-law and mother-in-law Daddy John Oyewopo and Mummy Deborah Oyewopo, you are the parents I have now. Thank you for your prayers and words of encouragement. Mummy Oyewopo, you are a great praying woman of God, and I am so grateful to you.

To my sons King David Boluwatife Abisoye Oyewopo and Father Abraham Adekolade Ayodeji

Oyewopo, I am grateful to you both. I thank you for your encouragement and daily support. I am so proud to be called your mother.

To my precious siblings Pastor Adedoyin Osikoya, Adeleke Osikoya, Abolanle Idris, Taiwo Osikoya and Oluwafunmito Osikoya. I am very grateful to you all. Family is great; you are all great people in my life. Thank you all for our childhood. It is one beautiful memory I can never forget and will not trade for anything.

To all my spiritual fathers and mothers, thank you for your deposits of wisdom and grace in my life. Your teachings shaped my world view. You feed me with the eternal Word of God. Day and night, you all labored on me. I am grateful to each of you.

To all my friends, thank you so much for your support and friendship, which I really appreciate. You have all been good role models to me. Your lives have challenged me.

To my brothers-in-law and sisters-in-law, I love you all and appreciate your prayers for me. Thank you so much.

FOREWORD

When you've experienced a conviction that has transformed your life for good, you can't help but share it. The propelling truth in your heart, bubbling with so much joy, carries the hope that others will experience the same transformation and more. However, sharing that testimony for the world to see, feel, and touch in the form of writing, speaks volumes of the power that a personal conviction truly has.

The Glorious Woman, written by Dotun Oyewopo, highlights how obeying the word of God brings stability, growth and fulfilment in all areas of a female's life. In the years I have known Dotun, her passion for uplifting ladies has been obvious. Yet, her hunger and vision to see women understand their divine calling in God's plan, is further evident in the writing. The book, *The Glorious Woman*, beautifully displays the courage, humility and inner beauty that can be encapsulated in the females of today.

As I read the pages, the honesty, nobility and purity of the prayers at the end of every chapter, exposed the areas of my life where I have been complacent. It challenged my daily walk to please God, but it also strengthened me in a refreshing way.

As an everyday woman, life can get very, very busy. You're often required to wear many different hats in a single day to suit whatever role you must play in the moment. However, this book reminded me that regardless of how hectic the world gets around me, there are some things that just cannot be compromised. Therefore, I am grateful for the truth that is emphasized throughout the book. Your title as a 'woman', comes with its roles and responsibilities.

The Glorious Woman details step by step, what God says about you and provides targeted scriptures as encouragement. It covers the positive influence you can be as a 'glorious woman' in all aspects of life, including your marriage, children, career, and ministry. As well as this, it outlines the processes that will build you up, and guides you with some of the prayers you'll need in this walk.

Dear Woman, where you are today physically, mentally, socially, and spiritually, is largely a reflection of the decisions and choices you have made, whether you believe it or not. I encourage you to read *The Glorious Woman* and make the choice to enjoy and accept the transformation it will bring into your life. Dotun Oyewopo has made the choice to share with you the blessings and impact encompassed in pursuing the journey of a glorious woman.

Baribela Idris

REVIEWS

The book glorious woman is easy to read. Love the scriptures and the prayers at the end of each chapter. I will recommend this book for all women.

Pastor Gladys Boadi

The book, *"The Glorious Woman"*, is all about the woman that brings glory to God in all her daily endeavor in order to please the master her maker and enjoy a blissful eternity. My favorite part of this book is chapter two which dwells on the nine attributes of the glorious woman. This book will grip you and keep you yearning to search the scriptures more. I will recommend this book for young women and all virtuous women who are on the pathway of a glorious journey to heaven. Thanks.

Bunmi Omodunbi

Pastor Dotun is a seasoned woman of God, a fantastic wife and a wonderful mother. She is full of positive energy, joy and the inspiration of the Holy

Spirit. She is willing to share same with every reader of this book "Glorious Woman". Having read through the pages of this book written by an experienced woman of God, I must say that this book is a pure blessing to every reader.

The book, *"The Glorious Woman"* by Pastor Dotun Oyewopo is a combination of intense research and the inspiration of the Holy Spirit. It highlights how God can repackage and upgrade a woman and re-introduce her to her world in a unique way that the world will marvel at what God can fashion out of a woman. Audacity and modesty are very well consolidated in a glorious woman. Doing everyday life with God on her side, a glorious lady can function successfully in distinctive roles. Each chapter concludes with a prayer which is another source of strength for a noblewoman. Dear reader, the glory that God wants to reveal in you is uncommon. It is more than elegant gold ornaments, hairstyle or clothes; it emanates from your heart and radiates from inside out. Outward beauty can fade, but inner beauty endures, Christ in you the hope of glory. I am convinced that reading this book is a good choice, you will be glad you did.

Pastor Kehinde Adigun.

It's really very interesting and informative. Much recommended to every woman whether or not the person is a believer. I like in particular the prayer sections, the self-reflections and the invitation to accept Christ at the back of the book. You are really blessed and this book will bless many women of all ages. Please send me a copy once it's out.

Dr Rayo Adebayo.

Dotun Oyewopo's *"The Glorious Woman"* is a simple, easy to read and understand book for all women across all ages and stages. The author is a well-respected and educated woman of God. Her book made me assess my current expression of His beauty/glory in comparison to His word. I encourage you to read this book, it will make you a better woman and help you train your daughters to express God's beauty in the different areas of their lives. Her seven ways to let go of past hurts is a useful gift to yourself and others.

Dr Tomi Kuteyi Ibilola

Wow! Very good book, keeps the reader interested. Perfect book for women empowerment, young and old alike. Recommended for ladies group studies as it triggers points of discussion and gives on point bible reference for conclusions. Well done Pastor Dotun, my dear friend.

Hope Kachila

The glorious woman is a ministering tool. A book that reminds us that as women we need the inner glow; which only comes from continually being in the presence of God. A great read. I highly recommend.

Kudzai Magaya Chibanda.

HOW TO USE THIS BOOK

This book is about the glorious woman. According to the Bible, glory is elevated from one level to another; hence, we can become transformed from one level of glory to another. That means no matter what your current level is as a glorious woman, there is definitely room for improvement.

This book has the potential to transform your life to the next level of glory if you will allow it. You need to know there are two parts of knowledge:

1. Information
2. Application

Interestingly, it is the application part that leads to life transformation. Therefore, I have provided application tools and worksheets in this book to help you apply the information therein.

STEPS TO MAXIMISE THE POTENTIAL OF THE BOOK

1. Read the chapters
2. Pray the prayer at the end of each chapter

3. Use the "Wheel of Glory" to assess where you are as per the information in the chapter
4. Commit to making changes in your life
5. Use the Action Plan Worksheet to create action plans that will help you progress from where you are to where you want to be in life.
6. Go ahead and implement your plans.

CONTENTS

Acknowledgment

Foreword

How to Use This Book

CHAPTER ONE
Who is A Glorious Woman? 25

CHAPTER TWO
The Two Types of Glory................................32

CHAPTER THREE
Attributes of a Glorious Woman 41

CHAPTER FOUR
19 Facts about a Glorious Woman? 55

CHAPTER FIVE
Self-Worth of the Glorious Woman....................61

CHAPTER SIX
Four Dimensions of Glory..............................67

CHAPTER SEVEN
Spiritual Glory...71

CHAPTER EIGHT
Mental Glory – Wisdom..............................107

CHAPTER NINE
Emotional Glory......................................133

CHAPTER TEN
Physical Glory..149

CHAPTER ELEVEN
Confessions of the Glorious Woman..................161

CHAPTER TWELVE
Prayer of Transformation 165

How to be Saved 171

THE GLORY OF GOD

The glory of God is the beauty of His Spirit. It is not a material beauty. It does not mean riches or power, but it is the beauty that emanates from His character and all that He is. This glory can crown man or fill the earth.

It has been called the manifested presence of God but more than being just a presence, it is a power. The kind of power that resurrects, delivers, overcomes, and transforms. It is greater and stronger than any other power in existence. And it belongs to us as glorious women.

It belongs to you as a glorious woman to transform your life, marriage, work, children, ministry, business, and career.

Our Lord Jesus is the king of all glory, and He has made us co-heirs with Him. Arise, glorious woman! Enjoy what belongs to you in Christ Jesus.

To Your Success
Dotun Oyewopo

Chapter One

WHO IS A GLORIOUS WOMAN?

According to Cambridge dictionary, the word **"glorious"** means, very beautiful, deserving great admiration, praise, honour and giving great pleasure.

> WHEN YOU MANIFEST GLORY, YOU AUTOMATICALLY ENJOY HONOUR. GLORY AND HONOUR GO TOGETHER.

According to Collins dictionary, the word **"glorious"** means, impressive, splendid, beautiful, bright, brilliant, delightful, fine, wonderful, excellent, illustrious, famous, celebrated, distinguished.

WHO IS A GLORIOUS WOMAN?

A glorious woman is a woman who shines brightly with light. She is that woman marked by great beauty or splendour. She is clearly different in her attitudes, behaviours and how she presents herself. She is that woman who is notable, brilliant, and outstanding.

God has called her to be glorious, to display His beauty and splendour, to shine brightly and manifest His glory in her home, life, ministry, and family. God wants the world to see all these excellent qualities in her. The beauty and splendour spoken of in the scriptures are not just outward or fading characteristics. Rather, it talks about the undying beauty of Christ in her that is the true hope of

> A GLORIOUS WOMAN'S HONOUR AND PRAISE ARE NOT IN SELF-GLORY BUT IN THE GOD OF GLORY.

glory. As women, when we say yes to God, we are washed, cleansed, and purified by His life-changing Word and the power of His Spirit. God takes us from glory to glory.

A glorious woman's honour and praise are not in self-glory but in the God of glory. Her lifestyle brings praise to her God, home, husband, children, and church. When people see this glorious woman, they give glory to God for her life.

Glory can also mean honour. When you manifest glory, you automatically enjoy honour. Glory and honour go together. Honour can be defined as respect, regard, and value.

Husbands, love your wives, just as Christ loved the church and gave himself up for her to make her holy, cleansing her by the washing with water through the word, and to present her to himself as a radiant church, without stain or wrinkle or any other blemish, but holy and blameless. **(Ephesians 5:25-27).**

THE GLORIOUS WOMAN

Charm is deceptive, and beauty is fleeting; but a woman who fears the Lord is to be praised
(Proverbs 31:30).

To them God has chosen to make known among the Gentiles the glorious riches of this mystery, which is Christ in you, the hope of glory
(Colossians 1:27).

PRAYERS

Father, help me to be a glorious woman. I acknowledge the fact that I cannot be one without Your help. Let Your glory be my light, and let my light shine brightly for the world to see Your great beauty and splendour in my home, life, ministry, and family.

Father, let Your glory be notable in me. Let it make me brilliant and outstanding everywhere I go. Father, help me to live a lifestyle that brings praise to You, my home, husband, children, and church. Help me to correct whatever is in my life that will bring shame to You.

Father, teach me how to continually live in Your glory. Let me not fall short of Your glory. Help me to deal with anything in my life that will repeal Your glory.

Father, take me from glory to glory. Let Your glory be my light.

Father, let Your glory bring honour into my life. In Jesus' name, I pray.

Chapter Two

THE TWO TYPES OF GLORY

YOUR BEAUTY should not come from OUTWARD ADORNMENT, such as elaborate hairstyles and the wearing of gold jewellery or fine clothes. Rather, it should be that of your INNER SELF, the unfading beauty of a gentle and quiet spirit, which is of GREAT WORTH in God's sight **(1 Peter 3-4).**

The focus of a woman's glory should be on her inner self, not her outward appearance. The scripture above shows us two types of glory: the inner glory and the outward glory. God wants us to be beautiful as women, but He also wants us to know the difference between the inner and outer glory. In the verse, Peter advises women that their beauty should not come from outward adornment but from the inner self-adornment.

> GOD WANTS US TO BE BEAUTIFUL AS WOMEN, BUT HE ALSO WANTS US TO KNOW THE DIFFERENCE BETWEEN THE INNER AND OUTER GLORY.

Charm is deceptive, and beauty does not last; but a woman who fears the LORD will be greatly praised. **(Proverbs 31:30, NLT)**

WHAT IS INNER AND OUTER GLORY?

According to the Word of God, inner glory is "the unfading beauty of a gentle and quiet spirit, which is of great worth in God's sight". Inner glory is also a deep respect and fear of the Lord which manifests in thoughts, words and behaviour.

THE TWO TYPES OF GLORY

Outward glory or adornment is "such as elaborate hairstyles and the wearing of gold jewellery or fine clothes."

Peter's emphasis was on getting women to focus on the importance of inner beauty above outer beauty. Moreover, God always looks at our hearts, not the clothes and jewellery we wear or the riches we have. God is not impressed or influenced by our material possessions or physical appearances. It is not just the good deeds you do that make you beautiful, but your gentle, quiet spirit and pure heart make you shine.

> **IT IS NOT JUST THE GOOD DEEDS YOU DO THAT MAKE YOU BEAUTIFUL, BUT YOUR GENTLE, QUIET SPIRIT AND PURE HEART MAKE YOU SHINE.**

When they arrived, Samuel saw Eliab and thought, "Surely the Lord's anointed stands here before the Lord." But the Lord said to Samuel, "DO NOT CONSIDER his APPEARANCE or his HEIGHT, for I have rejected him. The Lord does not look at the things people look at. People look at the OUTWARD

APPEARANCE, but the Lord looks at the heart **(1 Samuel 16:6-7).**

In 1 Samuel Chapter 16:7, Eliab was tall and handsome; yet, God rejected him, even though Samuel approved of him because of his physical stature. God made His choice and preferences clear to us. *HE LOOKS AT THE HEART.*

Jesse had seven of his sons pass before Samuel, but Samuel said to him, "The LORD has not chosen these." So he asked Jesse, "Are these all the sons you have?" "There is still the youngest," Jesse answered. "He is tending the sheep." Samuel said, "Send for him; we will not sit down until he arrives." So he sent for him and had him brought in. He was glowing with health and had a fine appearance and handsome features. Then the LORD said, "Rise and anoint him; this is the one." So Samuel took the horn of oil and anointed him in the presence of his brothers, and from that day on the Spirit of the LORD came powerfully upon David. Samuel then went to Ramah **(1 Samuel 16:10-13).**

THE TWO TYPES OF GLORY

In 1 Samuel 16:12, God approved David because of his inner qualities.

WOMEN FOCUS MORE ON THE OUTWARD ADORNMENT

Many women focus on their outward adornment; they are very concerned about how they look on the outside because that's what people can see. However, the Bible clearly states that your physical beauty is not the most important aspect of who you are. A lot of women place greater value on clothes, shoes, bags, cars, and jewellery than on the Holy Spirit inside them. Of course, it is easy to boast about the trappings and riches we have, but that is not what God sees as most significant when He looks at us.

> OUR FOCUS MUST BE ON PLEASING OUR GOD AND PAYING MORE ATTENTION TO WHAT IS OF GREAT WORTH TO HIM.

We have to careful not to fall for the tricks of the Devil. Our focus must be on pleasing our God and paying more attention to what is of great worth to

Him. One of the problems of shifting our focus from inside to outside is the possibility that pride will come. We boast about all the things we have forgetting that they will perish, instead of boasting about knowing God.

But let the one who boasts boast about this: that they have the understanding to know me, that I am the Lord, who exercises kindness, justice and righteousness on earth, for in these I delight," declares the Lord

(Jeremiah 9:24).

Therefore, as it is written: "Let the one who boasts boast in the Lord

(1 Corinthians 1:31).

But, "Let the one who boasts, boast in the Lord." For it is not the one who commends himself who is approved, but the one whom the Lord commends.

(2 Corinthians 10:17-18).

THE TWO TYPES OF GLORY

SELF-GLORY

Self-glory is the act of glorying in the flesh. That is, taking great pride and pleasure in one's wisdom and riches. It is to boast of one's self rather than giving the glory to God. God does not want anybody to share His glory with Him. Furthermore, He does not like the proud heart. If the Spirit of God dwells in your heart, there will be no place for pride. It is important to recognise that self-glory is temporary; it is like the flower that withers away. Riches and the flesh do not last forever.

> SELF-GLORY IS THE ACT OF GLORYING IN THE FLESH. THAT IS, TAKING GREAT PRIDE AND PLEASURE IN ONE'S WISDOM AND RICHES.

Your heart became proud on account of your beauty, and you corrupted your wisdom because of your splendour. So I threw you to the earth; I made a spectacle of you before kings

(Ezekiel 28:17).

THE GLORIOUS WOMAN

For, All people are like grass, and all their glory is like the flowers of the field; the grass withers and the flowers fall.

(1 Peter 1:24).

THE TWO TYPES OF GLORY

PRAYERS

Father, Let Your glory shine in me. Let my beauty not only be from outward adornment. Help me not to concentrate on my jewellery as the source of my beauty.

Father, Make me a woman with the inner beauty that is unfading and gentle.

Father, Make me a woman with a quiet spirit. Make me a woman with the type of inner beauty that is great and worthy in Your sight.

Father, Help me to know when to stop giving much attention to my outward looks. Let my boast be in You my Lord. Help me not to commend myself for Your approval. Commend me, Lord. Let my boast be that I know my God and His wondrous ways.

Father, I pray that I will not glory in my wisdom. I will give You all the glory You deserve. Lord, teach me to know the difference between the inner and outer glory.

THE GLORIOUS WOMAN

Father, Give me the unfading beauty of a gentle and quiet spirit, which is of great worth in God's sight. Lord, wash, cleanse, and purify my life with Your life-changing Word.

In Jesus' name, I pray.

Chapter Three

THE ATTRIBUTES OF A GLORIOUS WOMAN

1. A GLORIOUS WOMAN SEEKS GOD FIRST

The glorious woman must reject the lie that anything or anyone else should take preference over God. God must be the

THE GLORIOUS WOMAN

number one priority in everything she does. Her husband, children, and job come after God. She must strive daily to be obedient. God wants us as glorious women to seek Him first. In return, He has promised to bless us with all the things we need in our homes, marriages, businesses, families, and ministries.

> FOR A GLORIOUS WOMAN TO DO THE EXTRAORDINARY, SHE MUST KNOW HER GOD LIKE QUEEN ESTHER DID.

But seek first his kingdom and his righteousness, and all these things will be given to you as well.
(Matthew 6:33).

The lions may grow weak and hungry, but those who seek the LORD lack no good thing **(Psalm 34:10).**

But if from there you seek the LORD your God, you will find him if you seek him with all your heart and with all your soul. When you are in distress and all these things have happened to you, then in later days you will return to the LORD your God and obey him. For the LORD your God is a merciful God; he will not abandon or destroy you or forget the covenant with your ancestors, which he confirmed to them by oath.

(Deuteronomy 4:29-31).

2. A GLORIOUS WOMAN MUST KNOW HER GOD

For a glorious woman to do the extraordinary, she must know her God like Queen Esther did. Esther knew her God to the point where she said, "If I perish I perish." However, she did not perish because God delivered her, and the king granted her request. A glorious woman must know God's ways and deeds.

But the people that do know their God shall be strong and do exploits.

(Daniel 11:32b).

He made known his ways to Moses, his deeds to the people of Israel.

(Psalm 103:7).

3. A GLORIOUS WOMAN MUST TRUST GOD

A glorious woman needs to trust God with her heart, mind, mouth, body, and emotions. She must put her absolute trust in the almighty God who has revealed Himself to us through the Holy Bible, which is a book telling us about Himself. This great book is the Word of God. As you get to know Him through His Word by reading it and meditating on it, you will begin to see that He is absolutely trustworthy; hence, your trust in Him will grow. Many people in the Bible trusted God in various situations, and He did not fail them.

Great women in the Bible stood on the Word of God, and He honoured them. When it seemed as if nothing was happening, they did not stop trusting in God. Sarah trusted God for Isaac; Hannah trusted God for Samuel, and Esther trusted God for the deliverance of the children of Israel. God answered all their prayers. As you put your trust in God, He will show you great and mighty things.

> MANY PEOPLE IN THE BIBLE TRUSTED GOD IN VARIOUS SITUATIONS, AND HE DID NOT FAIL THEM.

Those who trust in the LORD are like Mount Zion, which cannot be shaken but endures forever.
(Psalm 125:1).

But blessed is the one who trusts in the Lord, whose confidence is in him. They will be like a tree planted by the water that sends out its roots by the stream. It does not fear when heat comes; its leaves are always green. It has no worries in a year of drought and never fails to bear fruit
(Jeremiah 17:7-8).

But those who hope in the Lord will renew their strength. They will soar on wings like eagles, they will run and not grow weary, they will walk and not be faint.
(Isaiah 40:31).

4. A GLORIOUS WOMAN MUST FEAR GOD

"Many women do noble things, but you surpass them all." Charm is deceptive, and beauty is fleeting; but a woman who fears the Lord is to be praised.
(Proverbs 31: 29-30).

The beauty of this great woman in Proverbs 31 is that she fears the Lord. The Proverbs 31 woman focused on pleasing her God. She was neither ready to please people nor was she proving her superpower. All she wanted to do was fear her God.

If you want to be like this glorious woman, you must learn to fear and honour God. When you do so, you will be a woman to be praised by God.

The Bible says that any woman who fears the Lord is to be praised. This great woman got the entire chapter of Proverbs 31 written about herself because she feared the Lord. Physical beauty has always been the world's standard of measuring a woman, but each time I read Proverbs 31:29-30, "Many daughters have done noble things, but you surpass them all! Charm is deceptive and beauty is fleeting, but a woman who fears the LORD is to be praised" I am reminded that charm

> PHYSICAL BEAUTY HAS ALWAYS BEEN THE WORLD'S STANDARD OF MEASURING A WOMAN, BUT....CHARM AND BEAUTY ARE NOT GOD'S CRITERIA FOR JUDGING US AS WOMEN.

THE ATTRIBUTES OF A GLORIOUS WOMAN

and beauty are not God's criteria for judging us as women; we are not bound by them. The Proverbs 31 woman found her freedom by fearing the Lord. A glorious woman is totally free when she commits herself to be God's woman.

For a glorious woman to operate in the realm of wisdom, knowledge, and understanding, the fear of the Lord must be in her heart and God has to be the central focus of her life.

The fear of the Lord is the beginning of wisdom, and knowledge of the Holy One is understanding.
(Proverbs 9:10).

Blessed are all who fear the Lord, who walk in obedience to him. You will eat the fruit of your labor; blessings and prosperity will be yours. Your wife will be like a fruitful vine within your house; your children will be like olive shoots

> FOR A GLORIOUS WOMAN TO OPERATE IN THE REALM OF WISDOM ... THE FEAR OF THE LORD MUST BE IN HER HEART.

around your table. Yes, this will be the blessing for the man who fears the Lord.

(Psalm 128:1-4).

Whoever fears the Lord has a secure fortress, and for their children it will be a refuge. The fear of the Lord is a fountain of life, turning a person from the snares of death.

(Proverbs 14:26-27)

5. A GLORIOUS WOMAN MUST HONOUR GOD

To honour God means to fear and reverence Him. When we honour God, we are glorifying Him. As a glorious woman, you honour God by doing what pleases Him in everything you do and with everything you have. Your life must attract honour to God. It is not enough to merely honour Him outwardly. He desires honour that comes from our hearts.

The Lord says, 'These people come near to me with their mouth and honour me with their lips, but

their hearts are far from me. Their worship of me is based on merely human rules they have been taught
(Isaiah 29:13).

Let all the earth fear the Lord; let all the people of the world revere him. For he spoke, and it came to be; He commanded, and it stood firm
(Psalm 33:8-9).

Flee from sexual immorality. All other sins a person commits are outside the body, but whoever sins sexually, sins against their own body. Do you not know that your bodies are temples of the Holy Spirit, who is in you, whom you have received from God? You are not your own; you were bought at a price. Therefore honor God with your bodies.
(1 Corinthians 6:18-20).

6. A GLORIOUS WOMAN MUST OBEY GOD

The glorious woman must trust, submit, and surrender to God and His Word. She must obey God because God blesses and rewards obedience.

And through your descendants all the nations of the

earth will be blessed-all because you have obeyed me

(Genesis 22:18).

But don't just listen to God's word. You must do what it says. Otherwise, you are only fooling yourselves. For if you listen to the word and don't obey, it is like glancing at your face in a mirror. You see yourself, walk away, and forget what you look like. But if you look carefully into the perfect law that sets you free, and if you do what it says and don't forget what you heard, then God will bless you for doing it. If you claim to be religious but don't control your tongue, you are fooling yourself, and your religion is worthless.

(James 1:22–25).

7. A GLORIOUS WOMAN MUST SERVE GOD

Each one should use whatever gift he has received to serve others, faithfully administering God's grace in its various forms. If anyone speaks, he should do it as one speaking the very words of God. If anyone serves, he should do it with the strength God provides, so that in all things God may be praised through Jesus Christ. To him be the glory and the power forever and ever Amen.

(1 Peter 4:10-11).

As women, we have received our gifts from God for two main purposes:
1. To bring glory to the name of God through our service
2. To serve others

Our service is not done to call attention to ourselves. We serve so that the name of God is glorified. Every glorious woman must set her mind on eternal things. She must serve the eternal King and live to please only Him.

But if serving the LORD seems undesirable to you, then choose for yourselves this day whom you will serve, whether the gods your ancestors served beyond the Euphrates, or the gods of the Amorites, in whose land you are living. But as for me and my household, we will serve the LORD

(Joshua 24:15).

Anyone who loves their life will lose it, while anyone who hates their life in this world will keep it for eternal life. Whoever serves me must follow me; and where I am, my servant also will be. My Father will honour the one who serves me **(John 12:25-26).**

8. A GLORIOUS WOMAN MUST PLEASE GOD

A glorious woman must seek to please God, not man. She must strive to do so in all her ways. She must have faith in the Word of God, and do the will of the Father. How can a glorious woman please God?

- Living a life of obedience
- Living a righteous life
- Doing the will of the Father

But without faith it is impossible to please Him, for he who comes to God must believe that He is and that He is a rewarder of those who diligently seek Him **(Hebrews 11:6).**

9. A GLORIOUS WOMAN MUST WORSHIP GOD

God desires worshippers who worship in spirit and

truth. We must worship God like Mary of Bethany who anointed Jesus' feet with a costly perfume. Worship brings transformation.

We were created for intimacy with God. However, sometimes we let situations; problems and other factors prevent us from reaching that point of intimacy. Our worship must have real meaning to God. Worship takes us to a place of truth and openness.

> **WE WERE CREATED FOR INTIMACY WITH GOD.**

PRAYERS

Father, help me to seek You in all my ways and make You my priority. Help me to seek You first, so I can enjoy your blessings. Lord, help me to know You like Queen Esther did. Help me to know Your ways and deeds.

Help me to put my trust in You and Your words. As I put my trust in You, Lord, let me encounter Your great power of possibilities. Lord, let Your fear be in my heart.

The Bible says the fear of the Lord is the beginning of wisdom. A woman who fears the Lord shall be praised. In Your fear, Lord, there is strong confidence. Help me to honour You with all I am and all I have.

Father, help me to obey You in all I do, serve You with my gifts, and please You by doing your will. Lord, help me to worship you in truth and in spirit.
In Jesus' name, I pray.

Chapter Four

19 FACTS ABOUT A GLORIOUS WOMAN

- **A GLORIOUS WOMAN IS REASONABLE.**

She is fair-minded and open to reason. She has a good sense of judgment.

- **A GLORIOUS WOMAN IS GENEROUS.**

She is not selfish. She willingly gives to others.

- **A GLORIOUS WOMAN IS RESPECTFUL.**

She is courteous. She has regard for others, and she is polite.

- **A GLORIOUS WOMAN IS GENUINE.**

She stands by what she says. She is very straightforward in her ways and words.

- **A GLORIOUS WOMAN IS A GOOD LISTENER.**

She gives a listening ear to others. She pays attention to the needs of others.

- **A GLORIOUS WOMAN IS HELPFUL.**

She gives a helping hand to others. She supports them as much as she can.

- **A GLORIOUS WOMAN IS KNOWLE- DGEABLE.**

She is well-informed on different issues.

- **A GLORIOUS WOMAN IS CONFIDENT.**

She is self-reliant. She believes in herself and carries herself with pride.

- **A GLORIOUS WOMAN IS COURAGEOUS.**

She is fearless. She can face any challenge that comes her way. She is very bold.

19 FACTS ABOUT A GLORIOUS WOMAN

- A GLORIOUS WOMAN IS INSIGHTFUL

She has the ability to discern. This is a gift from God. She shows good understanding on issues.

- A GLORIOUS WOMAN IS VISIONARY.

She thinks creatively, and she can see the future with her imagination.

- A GLORIOUS WOMAN IS MERCIFUL

She is willing to forgive others. She is ready to let go of offences.

- A GLORIOUS WOMAN IS HUMBLE.

She is very modest; she is not proud or arrogant.

- A GLORIOUS WOMAN IS MODEST.

She is not boastful.

- A GLORIOUS WOMAN IS IMAGINATIVE.

She is very creative.

- A GLORIOUS WOMAN IS INCREDIBLE.

She is good at many things.

THE GLORIOUS WOMAN

- **A GLORIOUS WOMAN IS INDUSTRIOUS.**

She is very hardworking and energetic.

- **A GLORIOUS WOMAN IS AN INITIATOR.**

She starts things and makes them grow. She initiates good and godly ideas.

- **A GLORIOUS WOMAN IS INTERESTING.**

She is good at engaging others. She is very exciting to be with. People want to listen to her.

PRAYERS

Father, help me to be a woman open to reason. Give me the grace not to think about myself alone; help me not to be selfish. Help me to be courteous in all my ways.

Father, help me to be true in all my ways and words and to be there for others to pay attention to them. Teach me how to face the challenges of life. Make me a bold woman.

Father, help me to be creative and to show good understanding in all I say and do. Show me Your mercy as I show others mercy. Let my boast be in You. Help me to be hard working.

In Jesus' name . Amen

Chapter Five

THE SELF-WORTH OF A GLORIOUS WOMAN

It is true that we are in this world, but we are not of this world. God told us that there is someone called the god of this age, the Devil who has blinded the unbelievers, so they cannot see.

The god of this age has blinded the minds of unbelievers, so that they cannot see the light of the gospel that displays the glory of Christ, who is the image of God. For what we preach is not ourselves, but Jesus Christ as Lord, and ourselves as your servants for Jesus' sake. For God, who said, "Let light shine out of darkness," made his light shine in our hearts to give us the light of the knowledge of God's glory displayed in the face of Christ **(2 Corinthians 4:4-6).**

The Devil blinds unbelievers preventing them from seeing the truth. However, as believers, we can see. Therefore, it is important that we see ourselves as Jesus sees us and not as the world sees us. We must believe in the light of God that shines in our hearts to give us the light of the knowledge of God's glory that is displayed in the face of Christ.

> YOUR IDENTITY IS FOUND IN THE WORD OF GOD THAT CAN NEVER FAIL. THIS IS THE TRUTH ABOUT WHO YOU ARE AND WHAT YOU ARE MADE OF.

THE SELF-WORTH OF A GLORIOUS WOMAN

As glorious women, our self-worth should be based on the light of the knowledge God has shone into our hearts through His Word. The Word of God has clearly defined who we are and who we are not. What we are and what we are not.

SCRIPTURE REVEALS WHO YOU ARE

As a glorious woman, your identity is found in Scripture, the word of God that can never fail. This is the truth about who you are and what you are made of. Nothing can change this. You are who God says you are, and you are what God says you are.

The Bible says you are not of this world; your kingdom is not on the earth. If you believe that you are a co-heir with our Lord Jesus Christ, then you must believe that this world cannot define you because the world does not know who you are. Hence, their definitions of

> YOU MUST BELIEVE THAT THIS WORLD CANNOT DEFINE YOU BECAUSE THE WORLD DOES NOT KNOW WHO YOU ARE.

you will surely be wrong.

Everything you need to know about yourself has been revealed to you by your heavenly Father in His Word. Scripture cannot be broken; it will only accomplish what it has been sent to do.

I pray that you will catch a revelation of who you are, and you will begin to live the dominion life you are meant to live rather than subjecting and lowering yourself to the standards of this world.

Then God said, 'Let us make mankind in our image, in our likeness, so that they may rule over the fish in the sea and the birds in the sky, over the livestock and all the wild animals, and over all the creatures that move along the ground.' God saw all that he had made, and it was very good. And there was evening, and there was morning—the sixth day **(Genesis 1:26, 31)**.

But you are a chosen people, a royal priesthood, a holy nation, God's special possession, that you may declare the praises of him who called you out of darkness into his wonderful light - **(1 Peter 2:9).**

For we are God's handiwork, created in Christ Jesus to do good works, which God prepared in advance for us to do - **(Ephesians 2:10).**

I said, 'You are "gods" you are all sons of the Most High.' - **(Psalm 82:6).**

I praise you because I am fearfully and wonderfully made; your works are wonderful, I know that full well - **(Psalm 139:14).**

Chapter Six
FOUR DIMENSIONS OF GLORY

And Jesus grew in wisdom and stature, and in favor with God and man. - **(Luke 2:52).**

Jesus is the king of glory. The preceding verse says He increased in wisdom, stature, and in favour with God and man. We can call these aspects of His growth the four dimensions of glory that our Lord Jesus manifested.

- Spiritual (in favour with God)

- Mental (increase in wisdom)
- Relational / emotional (in favour with men)
- Physical (increase in stature)

Every glorious woman must operate in these four dimensions of glory like Jesus. We must also manifest these four dimensions of glory. As women, we must increase spiritually, mentally, physically, and emotionally. I believe that with God, all things are possible. I believe that God has given us the grace to do all things.

I can do all this through him who gives me strength. - **(Philippians 4:13).**

Very truly I tell you, whoever believes in me will do the works I have been doing, and they will do even greater things than these, because I am going to the Father. And I will do whatever you ask in my name, so that the Father may be glorified in the Son. You may ask me for anything in my name, and I will do it. - **(John 14:12-14).**

In the following chapters, we will explore the four dimensions of glory for a glorious woman.

> AS GLORIOUS WOMEN, WE MUST INCREASE SPIRITUALLY, MENTALLY, PHYSICALLY, AND EMOTIONALLY.

Chapter Seven
SPIRITUAL GLORY

SPIRITUAL MATURITY

1. PRAYER

In the Bible, our Lord Jesus taught us how to pray. Many times, we read about Jesus praying to the Father. He did so at several crucial times in His life on the earth. For example, in the Garden of Gethsemane before His crucifixion and while He was dying on the cross. He also prayed before He chose His disciples.

The Bible tells us to pray without ceasing
- **(1 Thessalonians 5:16).**

It is a spiritual thing to do. God wants us to pray against every power of the Enemy in our homes, lives, marriages, businesses, and ministries. He promises that when we call upon Him, He will answer and show us great and mighty things
- **(Jeremiah 33:3).**

What an incredible promise! The infinite One, the Creator of the universe, the God of unlimited power and might invites us to call upon Him in our troubles.

> CRYING WILL NOT BRING THE SOLUTION WE WANT, ONLY PRAYERS CAN.

The Devil has come to steal, kill, and destroy
- **(John 10:10).**

Therefore, we have to pray against every negative plan he has concerning us. Prayer is very important, and we must intentionally create time to pray to God. Crying will not bring the solution we want, only prayers can. Someone said, "A closed mouth is a closed destiny."

Prayer is the heavenly language. The Devil knows this, and he will engage you to stop you from praying. Once you cannot pray, solutions will not come. Make up your mind today to build your prayer life. You are a soldier of Christ. Stand up and fight the good fight!

> "A CLOSED MOUTH IS A CLOSED DESTINY." STAND UP AND FIGHT THE GOOD FIGHT!

Call on Me in the day of trouble. I will take you out of trouble, and you will honor Me. **-(Psalm 50:15).**

Those who are right with the Lord cry, and He hears them. And He takes them from all their troubles **-(Psalm 34:17).**

I called to the Lord in my trouble. I cried to God for help. He heard my voice from His holy house. My cry for help came into His ears **- (Psalm 18:6).**

Come to me, all who labor and are heavy laden, and I will give you rest - **(Matthew 11:28).**

Then they cried out to the LORD in their trouble, and he brought them out of their distress. He stilled the storm to a whisper; the waves of the sea were hushed. They were glad when it grew calm, and he guided them to their desired haven

- **(Psalm 107:28-30).**

5 REASONS WHY YOU MUST PRAY

1. GOD CARES ABOUT YOU

God wants to show you how much He cares for you. He wants you to call on Him in your times of trouble. God wants you to know that He is not too busy to help you. You don't bother Him when you cast your burdens on Him. God never gets tired of hearing and meeting your needs.

> GOD TRULY DESIRES TO HELP US. HE WOULDN'T TELL US TO CALL UPON HIM IF HE WASN'T WILLING TO HELP US.

2. GOD WANTS TO HELP YOU

God truly desires to help us. He wouldn't tell us to call upon Him if He wasn't willing to help us. Remember the leper in Luke 5?

While Jesus was in one of the towns, a man came to Him with a bad skin disease over all his body. When he saw Jesus, he got down on his face before Him. He begged Him, saying, "Lord, if You are willing, You can heal me." Jesus put His hand on him and said, "I will, be healed." At once the disease went away from him - **(Luke 5:12-13).**

God is inclined to help us. He wants to do us good.

3. GOD KNOWS IT IS EASY FOR US TO PRAY TO HIM

All we need to do is to be willing, and we can pray to God. It is not a burden on us. We simply have to open our lips and lift up a whispered plea to the Lord. Anyone can call upon the Lord. It takes no training, skills, and no special talents. It takes but a minute.

God hears our everyday prayers. He is listening to us.

4. GOD PROMISES TO HEAR YOU WHEN YOU PRAY

God is a promise keeper. He never fails. He honours His word from generations to generations.

God promised, "I will deliver you." Therefore, we can be sure that He will not forget to deliver us. He will not change His mind or lie. He will hear us and come to our help to surely deliver us. It might not be on our timetable, but He will not fail to keep His word.

> **GOD IS A PROMISE KEEPER. HE NEVER FAILS. HE HONOURS HIS WORD FROM GENERATIONS TO GENERATIONS.**

God is not like people. He tells no lies. He is not like humans. He doesn't change his mind. When he says something, he does it. When he makes a promise, he keeps it - **(Numbers 23:19, GW).**

5. IT IS FOR HIS GLORY

All adoration goes to God after our victories. God receives the praise, honour, and glory. When He hears and helps us, it shows His faithfulness and unfailing love for us.

WOMAN OF FAITH

Faith is the power that connects us to the spiritual realm. It links us with God. God honours your faith. After praying, you must believe that God has done what you asked. Great men and women in the Bible exercised their faith, and God honoured them.

You must be a strong woman of faith, believe in your God, and have complete trust and confidence in Him to do what He has promised you. Your faith in God must be unshakable and strong.

A woman called Rahab had heard about the God of Israel, how powerful and

> YOUR FAITH IN GOD MUST BE UNSHAKABLE AND STRONG.

great He is. Thus, she decided to put her trust in Him. Her faith grew, and she believed that this God would deliver her. Rahab's faith in God brought great change to the story of the children of

Israel. They were able to conquer Jericho, and they entered the Promised Land.

Women like Sarah, Deborah, Hannah, Abigail, and the Shunammite woman all had faith in God, and He turned their stories around. Faith makes everything possible; therefore, be a woman of faith.

But without faith it is impossible to please him: for he that cometh to God must believe that he is, and that he is a rewarder of them that diligently seek him - **(Hebrews 11:6).**

Now faith is the substance of things hoped for, the evidence of things not seen - **(Hebrews 11:1).**

Against all hope, Abraham in hope believed and so became the father of many nations, just as it had been said to him, "So shall your offspring be. Without weakening in his faith, he faced the fact that his body was as good as dead—since he was about a hundred years old—and that Sarah's womb was also dead. Yet he did not waver through unbelief regarding the promise of God, but was strengthened in his faith and gave glory to God, being fully persuaded that God had power to do what he had promised. This is why "it was credited to him as righteousness." The words "it was credited to him" were written not for him alone, but also for us, to whom God will credit righteousness—for us who believe in him who raised Jesus our Lord from the dead. He was delivered over to death for our sins and was raised to life for our justification.

-**(Romans 4:18-25).**

WOMAN OF THE WORD

You must be a woman of the Word. The Bible says where the Word of God is, there is power.

Where the word of a king is, there is power: and who may say unto him, what doesn't thou?

- **(Ecclesiastes 8:4).**

The Word of God is powerful and everything responds to it, including the dead. Whatever the situation in your life, the Word of God can deal with it. Whatever battle you are fighting can be conquered with the Word of God that prevails over every storm of life.

If you have the Word of God, you already have the power to conquer. With the Word of God in your mouth, you can destroy every plan of the enemy. The Word of God spoken in faith in the name of Jesus has the awesome power to overcome any obstacles. If you have the Word of God in your mouth, then there is power in your home. All you need to do is to speak it. You don't have to worry about how it will work.

> THE WORD OF GOD IS POWERFUL AND STRONG. EVERYTHING RESPONDS TO IT, INCLUDING THE DEAD.

So is my word that goes out from my mouth: It will not return to me empty, but will accomplish what I desire and achieve the purpose for which I sent it - **(Isaiah 55:10-11).**

There is irresistible, supernatural power in God's Word; it will not return to Him empty. God's Word will accomplish His desires and purposes. The Bible says that the word of the Lord will not return empty to Him

In other words, it will get the job done! The Word of God is powerful because it is guaranteed by God to be effective. When you speak the Word of God, you are tapping into limitless power! The power you need is in the Word of God. Open your mouth and speak the Word over your situation.

> THERE IS IRRESISTIBLE, SUPERNATURAL POWER IN GOD'S WORD; IT WILL NOT RETURN TO HIM EMPTY. ....IT WILL GET THE JOB DONE!

WHY IS THE WORD OF GOD IMPORTANT?

- IT TAKES AWAY FEAR FROM YOU

In God, whose word I praise. In God I trust and am not afraid. What can mere mortals do to me?

- **(Psalm 56:4).**

- IT GIVES YOU LIGHT

The unfolding of your words gives light; it gives understanding to the simple - **(Psalm 119:130).**

- IT SHIELDS YOU

As for God, his way is perfect: The Lord's word is flawless; he shields all who take refuge in him

- **(Psalm 18:30).**

- IT SETS YOU FREE

To the Jews who had believed him, Jesus said, "If you hold to my teaching, you are really my disciples. Then you will know the truth, and the truth will set you free - **(John 8:31-32).**

BIBLE STUDY

The Bible is the Word of God. It contains the mind of God and His eternal will for us all as His children. The Bible was given to us to reveal the mind of God to us. It is the holy Word of God that has the total authority of God.

Forever, O LORD, Your word is settled in heaven - **(Psalm 119:89).**

When you study the Bible, you will begin to discover the authority that has been given to you as a child of God. This authority is divine, and it is backed by God's integrity. Studying the Bible helps you discover God's plan for your life.

All Scripture is given by inspiration of God, and is profitable for doctrine, for reproof, for correction, for instruction in righteousness, that the man of God may be complete, thoroughly equipped for every good work - **(2 Timothy 3:16-17).**

The only way you can find security in this life is by studying the Word of God.

So is my word that goes out from my mouth: It will not return to me empty, but will accomplish what I desire and achieve the purpose for which I sent it.

- **(Isaiah 55:11).**

As we study the Bible, we begin to see the promises of God. There are many promises in this great book for us as children of God. These promises give us hope and assurance in times of trials and temptations. Your life begins to change as the Word you study renews your mind. The Word of God is life to those who have found it and health to their flesh.

> THE ONLY WAY YOU CAN FIND SECURITY IN THIS LIFE IS BY STUDYING THE WORD OF GOD.

Do your best to present yourself to God as one approved, a worker who does not need to be ashamed and who correctly handles the word of truth. - **(2 Timothy 2:15).**

The Word of God that you know is the truth that will set you free. It is also what you are going to stand on to fight. If you don't study it, you can't know it, and if you don't know the Word of God, you cannot win your battles in life.

Keep this Book of the Law always on your lips; meditate on it day and night, so that you may be careful to do everything written in it. Then you will be prosperous and successful. - **(Joshua 1:8)**.

Your word is a lamp for my feet, a light on my path. - **(Psalm 119:105, ESV)**.

And now, brethren, I commend you to God, and to the word of his grace, which is able to build you up, and to give you an inheritance among all them which are sanctified - **(Acts 20:32)**.

WHY YOU NEED TO STUDY THE BIBLE

THE BIBLE GIVES YOU:
- Direction
- Guidance

- Clarity
- Good success
- It builds you up
- Gives you wisdom
- Corrects your wrong thinking
- Teaches you what is right
- Equips you for good work

GIFT OF THE HOLY SPIRIT

This is a special spiritual gift given by the Holy Spirit to every member of the body of Christ. You are a part of that body, and you have been given a special gift to function there. The Bible talks about the "divers gifts" of the Holy Spirit given to the church for the edification of the body of Christ, which is the church of God. You have different gifts given by the same Spirit.

As women, God has called us to different ministries but the same Lord. The manifestation

> YOU ARE A PART OF THAT BODY, AND YOU HAVE BEEN GIVEN A SPECIAL GIFT TO FUNCTION THERE.

of the Spirit through our gifts is given to profit all. If you don't know your gift, how can you profit the body of Christ?

There are different kinds of gifts, but the same Spirit distributes them. There are different kinds of service, but the same Lord. There are different kinds of working, but in all of them and in everyone it is the same God at work. Now to each one the manifestation of the Spirit is given for the common good. To one there is given through the Spirit a message of wisdom, to another a message of knowledge by means of the same Spirit, to another faith by the same Spirit, to another gifts of healing by that one Spirit, to another miraculous powers, to another prophecy, to another distinguishing between spirits, to another speaking in different kinds of tongues, and to still another the interpretation of tongues.

All these are the work of one and the same Spirit, and he distributes them to each one, just as he determines. - **(1 Corinthians 12:4-11).**

Your gift is for the edification of the body of Christ and also for your edification. As you use them, you will grow. I pray the Lord will open your eyes to know, see, and understand the great grace of God upon your life. Also that you will use your gift to its full capacity as the Lord has equipped you.

EXHIBIT THE FRUIT OF THE SPIRIT

Every glorious woman must exhibit the fruit of the Holy Spirit. God purposely specified the great nine fruits of the Holy Spirit. He is showing us the importance of these fruits, which come directly from the Holy Spirit, not from us.

As glorious women, we should do all we can in cooperation with the Holy Spirit to work these great fruits into our personalities.

- Love
- Joy
- Peace
- Forbearance

- Kindness
- Goodness
- Faithfulness
- Gentleness
- Self-control

These are God's divine attributes and personalities. With the help of the Holy Spirit, we share God's nature. As we grow in the Spirit, all the beautiful characteristics of our Lord Jesus Christ will be manifested in our lives. The Bible says there is no law against these nine fruits.

> **AS WE GROW IN THE SPIRIT, ALL THE BEAUTIFUL CHARACTERISTICS OF OUR LORD JESUS CHRIST WILL BE MANIFESTED IN OUR LIVES.**

But the fruit of the Spirit is love, joy, peace, forbearance, kindness, goodness, faithfulness, gentleness and self-control. Against such things there is no law - **(Galatians 5:22-23).**

It is important to allow the Holy Spirit to work in us so we can bear fruits. This is the only way we can overcome the works of the flesh. If we do not bear fruits then we will constantly struggle with sin

The acts of the flesh are obvious: sexual immorality, impurity and debauchery; idolatry and witchcraft; hatred, discord, jealousy, fits of rage, selfish ambition, dissensions, factions and envy; drunkenness, orgies, and the like. I warn you, as I did before, that those who live like this will not inherit the kingdom of God - **(Galatians 5:19-21).**

LIVING A RIGHTEOUS LIFE FOR GOD

The Bible says *"By their fruits you will recognize them."* **(Matthew 7:16).** You can't claim to be a child of God when you are not living according to His ways. A woman who claims to know God must work according to His will and her way of life must be the evidence of the Holy Spirit living in her.

SPIRITUAL GLORY

Living according to God's will mean that as a woman, you must not be involved in the following:

- Living by ungodly counsel
- Living by ungodly advice
- Cheating on your husband
- Lying
- Stealing
- Having ungodly relationships or friendships

To live a righteous life, you have to stand up and stand out. You cannot follow the lifestyles of the world that are in conflict with God's teachings. Therefore, you should be a woman of good character and integrity. You must be honest, decent, and full of morals.

> **TO LIVE A RIGHTEOUS LIFE, YOU HAVE TO STAND UP AND STAND OUT!**

Then you will understand what is right and just and fair every good path. - **(Proverbs 2:9).**

Flee from sexual immorality. All other sins a person commits are outside the body, but whoever sins sexually, sins against their own body. Do you not know that your bodies are temples of the Holy Spirit, who is in you, whom you have received from God? You are not your own; you were bought at a price. Therefore honour God with your bodies

- **(1 Corinthians 6:18-20).**

Or do you not know that wrongdoers will not inherit the kingdom of God? Do not be deceived: Neither the sexually immoral nor idolaters nor adulterers nor men who have sex with men nor thieves nor the greedy nor drunkards nor slanderers nor swindlers will inherit the kingdom of God. And that is what some of you were. But you were washed, you were sanctified, you were justified in the name of the Lord Jesus Christ and by the Spirit of our God - **(1 Corinthians 6:9-11).**

The acts of the flesh are obvious: sexual immorality, impurity and debauchery; idolatry and witchcraft; hatred, discord, jealousy, fits of rage, selfish ambition, dissensions, factions and envy; drunkenness, orgies, and the like. I warn you, as I did before, that those who live like this will not inherit the kingdom of God - **(Galatians 5:19-21).**

He went on: "What comes out of a person is what defiles them. For it is from within, out of a person's heart, that evil thoughts come—sexual immorality, theft, murder, adultery, greed, malice, deceit, lewdness, envy, slander, arrogance and folly. All these evils come from inside and defile a person

- **(Mark 7:20-23).**

Blessed is the one who does not walk in step with the wicked or stand in the way that sinners take or sit in the company of mockers, but whose delight is in the law of the LORD, and who meditates on his law day and night. That person is like a tree planted by streams of water, which yields its fruit in
- **(Psalm 1:1-6).**

SERVICE

Jesus taught us the truth about service. If you want to be the greatest, you must serve others. Jesus served His disciples by washing their feet.

There is always a great reward attached to service, and if you serve others with love and humility as Christ did, God will surely reward you. He will not forget your labour of love.

God is not unjust; he will not forget your work and the love you have shown him as you have helped his people and continue to help them - **(Hebrews 6:10).**

Let us not become weary in doing good, for at the proper time we will reap a harvest if we do not give up - **(Galatians 6:9).**

> THERE IS ALWAYS A GREAT REWARD ATTACHED TO SERVICE.

And, behold, I come quickly; and my reward is with me, to give every man according as his work shall be - **(Revelation 22:12).**

EVERY GLORIOUS WOMAN MUST:

- Serve God with her time
- Serve God with her talent
- Serve God with her money
- Serve her husband
- Serve her community
- Serve her country
- Serve her children
- Serve her church
- Serve her friends
- Be a good giver
- Be a good tither

REWARDS OF SERVICE

- **CROWN OF RIGHTEOUSNESS**

I have fought the good fight, I have finished the race, I have kept the faith. Now there is in store for me the crown of righteousness, which the Lord, the righteous Judge, will award to me on that day —

and not only to me, but also to all who have longed for his appearing - **(Timothy 4:7-8)**.

- REAP THE HARVEST

Let us not become weary in doing good, for at the proper time we will reap a harvest if we do not give up - **(Galatians 6:9)**.

- THEIR LABOUR IN THE LORD IS NOT IN VAIN

Therefore, my dear brothers, stand firm. Let nothing move you. Always give yourselves fully to the work of the Lord, because you know that your labour in the Lord is not in vain - **(1 Corinthians 15:58)**.

- REAP WITH SONGS OF JOY

Those who sow with tears will reap with songs of joy. Those who go out weeping, carrying seed to sow, will return with songs of joy, carrying sheaves with them **(Psalm 126:5-6,GW)**.

- HONOURED WITH THE PRESENCE OF CHRIST.

Father, I want those you have given me to be with me where I am, and to see my glory, the glory you have given me because you loved me before the creation of the world (John 17:24).

- ## HONOURED ON THE DAY OF JUDGMENT.

When the Son of Man comes in his glory, and all the angels with him, he will sit on his glorious throne. All the nations will be gathered before him, and he will separate the people one from another as a shepherd separates the sheep from the goats. He will put the sheep on his right and the goats on his left. Then the King will say to those on his right, 'Come, you who are blessed by my Father; take your inheritance, the kingdom prepared for you since the creation of the world - (Matthew 25:31-34).

- ## RECEIVE A PRICELESS INHERITANCE IN HEAVEN

And into an inheritance that can never perish, spoil or fade. This inheritance is kept in heaven for you, who through faith are shielded by God's power until the coming of the salvation that is ready to be revealed in the last time - (1 Peter 1:4-5).

- ## A KINGDOM WILL BE PREPARED FOR THEM IN HEAVEN

All the nations will be gathered before him, and he will separate the people one from another as a shepherd separates the sheep from the goats. He will put the sheep on his right and the goats on his left. "Then the King will say to those on his right, 'Come, you who are blessed by my Father; take your inheritance, the kingdom prepared for you since the creation of the world. For I was hungry and you gave me something to eat, I was thirsty and you gave me something to drink, I was a stranger and you invited me in, I needed clothes and you clothed me, I was sick and you looked after me, I was in prison and you came to visit me.' "Then the righteous will answer him, 'Lord, when did we see you hungry and feed you, or thirsty and give you something to drink? When did we see you a stranger and invite you in, or needing clothes and clothe you? When did we see you sick or in prison and go to visit you?' "The King will reply, 'Truly I tell you, whatever you did for one of the least of these brothers and sisters of mine, you did for me.' "Then he will say to those on his left, 'Depart from me, you who are cursed, into the eternal fire prepared for the devil and his angels. For I was hungry and you gave me nothing to eat, I was thirsty and you gave me nothing to drink, I was a stranger and you did not invite me in, I needed clothes and you did not clothe me, I was sick and in prison and you did not look after me.' "They also will answer, 'Lord, when did we see you hungry or thirsty or a stranger or needing clothes or sick or in prison, and did not help you? "He will reply, 'Truly I tell you, whatever you did not do for one of the least of these, you did not do for me.' "Then they will go away to eternal punishment, but the righteous to eternal life - **(Matthew 25:32-46).**

Every glorious woman who serves will definitely obtain a priceless inheritance in heaven. She will enjoy:

- Pleasure in heaven
- Rest from all her toil
- Peace from all conflicts
- Honour from all her shame

THE GLORIOUS WOMAN

- A beautiful crown for victory
- A scepter for conquest

SPIRITUAL GLORY

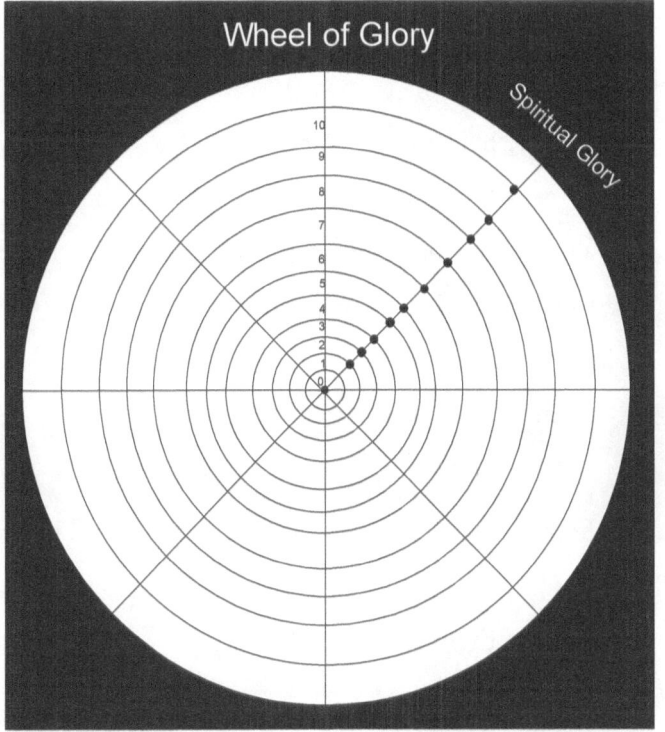

The diagram above is to help you see where you are on your journey.

Between 0 – 10, what score are you going to give yourself as related to attributes of Spiritual Glory? What specific spiritual attributes do you need to give attention to in your life? What are the required action steps that you need to take to be able to manifest full Spiritual Glory in your life?

PRAYERS

Father, help me to be a prayerful woman. Help me to grow my faith in You. Make me a woman of Your Word, so I can contact Your power. Help me to study and show myself approved, a woman who is not ashamed but rightly dividing the Word of truth.

Father, help me to grow in my ministry. This is my primary assignment. Help me to discover my gifts and use them for Your service.

Father, help me to continuously grow in the spirit and to manifest the fruit of the Holy Spirit so that Godly characters can be formed in me and manifested in my daily life.

Father, help me to live a life pleasing to You and to serve without complaining. Strengthen me to serve You with all You have given me.

Father, You reward greatly. Help me not to lose my rewards or fail You in the place of service. Enable me to serve wholeheartedly and let no one take my place so I can finish well.

In Jesus' name, I pray.

THE GLORIOUS WOMAN

ACTION PLAN SHEET

1. SET GOALS YOU WANT TO ACHIEVE IN THESE AREAS OF YOUR LIFE.

_____
_____
_____
_____

2. PUT A PLAN INTO PLACE ON HOW TO ACHIEVE YOUR GOALS.

_____
_____
_____
_____

3. LOOK FOR AREAS THAT NEED IMPROVEMENT IN ORDER FOR YOU TO ACHIEVE THESE GOALS.

_____
_____
_____
_____

4. LIST SCRIPTURES THAT YOU CAN STAND ON.

SPIRITUAL GLORY

_____
_____
_____
_____

Chapter Eight
MENTAL GLORY – WISDOM

In this chapter, we are going to talk about the mental glory of the glorious woman. What is expected of her mentally?

This chapter will be divided into three parts

1. Self-discovery
2. Entrepreneurship
3. Mental health

SELF-DISCOVERY

The American English Dictionary defines self-discovery as follows: "a becoming aware of one's true potential, character, motives, etc."

Self-discovery is very important to a glorious woman. It is the process of learning more about yourself and who you are. As we discuss self-discovery, we will look at four important areas a glorious woman needs to know more about and work on making better.

1. Personal development
2. Education
3. Financial education
4. Home maker

PERSONAL DEVELOPMENT

Personal development is an ongoing process of self-improvement. It is about setting goals for yourself

> SELF-DISCOVERY IS ....
> THE PROCESS OF LEARNING MORE ABOUT YOURSELF AND FINDING OUT WHO YOU ARE.

and putting plans in place to reach them. A glorious woman should always have in her mind that her sole responsibility is to intentionally develop herself.

She must add values to her life to be a better person. She must work towards whatever she considers valuable and useful for her.

- Learn a new skill
- Start a business

Six steps the glorious woman must take towards the personal development of others

- Inspire someone to be proactive
- Give a helping hand
- Encourage others when they are discouraged
- Listen to others
- Contribute to the education of others
- Teach new skills
- Add value to other people's lives

Six steps the glorious woman must take towards her personal development:

1. SHE MUST NOT BE STAGNATED MENTALLY

The glorious woman must not be stagnant mentally. Rather, she must always think big and create big visions for herself.

2. SHE MUST DEVELOP HER SKILLS

The glorious woman must not be tired of adding more value to her skills.

3. SHE MUST DEVELOP HER TALENTS

This is important because her talents are gifts from God. Putting them to use is not good enough. She must intentionally develop them and get better so she can serve others and be rewarded.

4. SHE MUST BE STUDIOUS

She must give attention to reading books. This will develop her mind and thinking. However, she should focus on reading books that will motivate and inspire her, not just any and every book.

5. SHE MUST ATTEND SEMINARS ONCE IN A WHILE

This will give her the opportunity to connect with people. It will also assist her in being well-informed.

Setting personal development goals is very important, but also remember that you should set goals that are achievable.

FOUR STEPS TO KEEP IN MIND AS YOU REACH OUT FOR YOUR PERSONAL DEVELOPMENT GOALS

1. Set goals you want to achieve in all areas of your life.

2. Look for areas that need improvement in order for you to achieve these goals.

3. Put a plan of action in place to improve these areas.

4. Create time for developing your strengths.

Enlarge the place of your tent, stretch your tent curtains wide, do not hold back; lengthen your cords, strengthen your stakes **(Isaiah 54:2).**

EDUCATION

This is an enlightening experience for any woman. It is very important that you continue to educate yourself because education creates many opportunities, and it builds your mind. It also gives you access to a lot of information and shapes your mindset.

> IT IS VERY IMPORTANT THAT YOU CONTINUE TO EDUCATE YOURSELF BECAUSE EDUCATION CREATES MANY OPPORTUNITIES, AND IT BUILDS YOUR MIND.

We must understand that people have different preferences and goals. Therefore, education means different things to different people. The most important thing is that whatever you do to educate yourself, do it well.

TYPES OF EDUCATION

We have 3 types of education

1. Formal

2. Informal

3. Non-formal – learning with the support of digital education where there is no direct involvement of teachers (self-help).

FINANCIAL EDUCATION

This is very important in every family. As a glorious woman, you must possess the skills and knowledge that allow you to make effective, sound decisions about the family finances.

Budgeting, family savings, investing and staying out of debt are very important. It gives you financial peace.

> BUDGETING, SAVING, INVESTING .. STAYING OUT OF DEBT .. GIVES YOU FINANCIAL PEACE.

GOOD HOMEMAKER

The glorious woman guides her home. God's plan for the woman is homemaking. There is no higher goal that a woman may desire or achieve. There is no nobler calling for her. God expects us to be good homemakers; thus, He has given us enough grace to do so.

To be self-controlled and pure, to be busy at home, to be kind, and to be subject to their husbands, so that no one will malign the word of God - **(Titus 2:5).**

NINE REWARDS OF A HOMEMAKER

1. SHE HAS THINGS GROWING AT HOME.
She considers a field and buys it; out of her earnings she plants a vineyard - **(Proverbs 31:16).**

2. SHE IS CALLED A VIRTUOUS WOMAN
A wife of noble character who can find? She is worth far more than rubies - **(Proverbs 31:10).**

3. SHE IS A WISE PURCHASER
She selects wool and flax and works with eager hands. She is like the merchant ships, bringing her food from afar - **(Proverbs 31:13-14).**

4. SHE IS PERSEVERING, HARD-WORKING

She sets about her work vigorously; her arms are strong for her tasks. She sees that her trading is profitable, and her lamp does not go out at night

-**(Proverbs 31:17-18).**

5. SHE IS COMPASSIONATE

She opens her arms to the poor and extends her hands to the needy. - **(Proverbs 31:20).**

6. SHE IS A GOOD COOK

She gets up while it is still night; she provides food for her family and portions for her female servants.

- **(Proverbs 31:15).**

7. SHE IS NEVER TAKEN BY SURPRISE; SHE IS EVER READY TO LOOK AFTER HER FAMILY

When it snows, she has no fear for her household; for all of them are clothed in scarlet. She makes coverings for her bed; she is clothed in fine linen and purple. - **(Proverbs 31:21-22).**

8. SHE IS PRAISED BY HER HUSBAND AND CHILDREN

Her children arise and call her blessed; her husband also, and he praises her. - **(Proverbs 31:38)**.

9. SHE IS A SUITABLE HELP TO HER HUSBAND; SHE ADDS VALUE TO HIS LIFE.

Her husband has full confidence in her and lacks nothing of value. She brings him good, not harm, all the days of her life - **(Proverbs 31:11-12)**.

ENTREPRENEURSHIP

Entrepreneurs are great people; they have extraordinary abilities. They can spot opportunities easily and quickly. They are full of great ideas and are very innovative. They build brands in their businesses. Just like any entrepreneur, the glorious woman must be creative, industrious and be able to spot opportunities for business. She must develop the entrepreneurship abilities in her.

> JUST LIKE ANY ENTREPRENEUR, THE GLORIOUS WOMAN MUST BE CREATIVE, INDUSTRIOUS AND BE ABLE TO SPOT OPPORTUNITIES FOR BUSINESS.

SHE IS NOT LAZY

The glorious woman is not lazy; she does her task very well.

She sets about her work vigorously; her arms are strong for her tasks - **(Proverbs 31:17).**

THE GLORIOUS WOMAN IS AN ENTREPRENEUR BY NATURE

She makes linen garments and sells them, and supplies the merchants with sashes.

- **(Proverbs 31:20).**

THE GLORIOUS WOMAN IS INDUSTRIOUS

Just like the Proverbs 31 woman, the glorious woman works hard for her family and also earns an income for them.

She looks at land and buys it, and with money she has earned she plants a vineyard (Proverbs 31:16).

MENTAL HEALTH

Mental health is a state of well-being where someone realises his or her own ability, can cope well with the stresses of life, and work productively. Mental health affects how we reason and feel; it also impacts our actions.

> MENTAL HEALTH AFFECTS HOW WE REASON AND FEEL; IT ALSO IMPACTS OUR ACTIONS.

SIGNS OF MENTAL HEALTH CONCERN

1. A change in character - someone acting differently

2. Lack of concern about appearance - this may be an indication of a mental health issue

3. Downheartedness - giving up on oneself, feeling that life is too hard and there is no hope

4. Segregation - spending too much time alone; this is a serious warning sign of emotional or mental health issues.

5. Severe changes in emotions - worry and anger are causes for alarm, especially if they are persistent.

If you are experiencing any of the signs above, you need to see a doctor.

We will take a look at the following under mental health as we continue:

1. Mindset
2. Wellbeing
3. Self-esteem
4. Right attitude

MINDSET

Our mindsets are our worldviews that can be changed because they are perspectives and powerful beliefs we have in our minds. If we change our minds, we can automatically change our mindsets.

> FOR YOU TO ACCOMPLISH ANYTHING GREAT IN LIFE, YOU HAVE TO TRUST YOURSELF AND BELIEVE IN YOUR GOD GIVEN CAPABILITIES.

As a glorious woman, you must have a positive mindset and use it to achieve your goals in life. For you to accomplish anything great in life, you have to trust yourself and believe in your capabilities. Your positive mindset is very important because it affects many aspects of your life. As a glorious woman, you must have the following:

- Positive mindset
- Brave mindset
- Informed mindset
- Fulfilling mindset
- Concentrated mindset
- Forgiving mindset

Do not conform to the pattern of this world, but be transformed by the renewing of your mind. Then you will be able to test and approve what God's will is - his good, pleasing and perfect will. **- (Romans 12:2).**

MENTAL GLORY - WISDOM

You were taught, with regard to your former way of life, to put off your old self, which is being corrupted by its deceitful desires; to be made new in the attitude of your minds. - **(Ephesians 4:22-23).**

WELLBEING

Wellbeing is not just the absence of disease or illness; it is a complex combination of a person's physical, mental, emotional, and social health factors. Wellbeing is strongly linked to happiness and life satisfaction. In short, wellbeing could be described as how you feel about yourself and your life.

> WELLBEING IS ... A COMPLEX COMBINATION OF A PERSON'S PHYSICAL, MENTAL, EMOTIONAL, AND SOCIAL HEALTH FACTORS.

Your wellbeing is extremely important if you desire to live a good quality life. You have to take care of yourself. Take a good look at where you are right now and be sincere to yourself. As a glorious woman, you ought to be full of life because God is your source of energy.

How is your wellbeing? If you need help please, don't hesitate to get it.

Do not be anxious about anything, but in every situation, by prayer and petition, with thanksgiving, present your requests to God. And the peace of God, which transcends all understanding, will guard your hearts and your minds in Christ Jesus.

-(Philippians 4:6-7).

SELF-ESTEEM

Self-esteem is the belief you have in yourself and your abilities. It is a sense of satisfaction you feel about who you are and your abilities. Your self-esteem is essential to your success; therefore, you should keep it at a high level. If you have low self-esteem, it will affect the way you see yourself, your relationships, family, work, social life, and almost everything you do. It can be so detrimental that it leads to depression. In fact, having low self-esteem stops you from

> LOW SELF-ESTEEM STOPS YOU FROM ACHIEVING MORE IN LIFE ... POSITIVE SELF-ESTEEM MOTIVATES YOU TO SUCCEED!

achieving more in life. On the other hand, positive self-esteem motivates you to succeed.

Remember, in Christ you live, move, and have your being. Our Lord Jesus Christ never had low self-esteem. He was confident in who He was and His mission on the earth. Likewise, we can be confident because we are created in the image of God, and we have the Holy Spirit in us.

I can do all things in Him who strengthens me
-(Philippians 4:13).

She is clothed with strength and dignity; she can laugh at the days to come.
-(Proverbs 31:25).

But by the grace of God I am what I am, and his grace to me was not without effect. No, I worked harder than all of them—yet not I, but the grace of

God that was with me. -(1 Corinthians 15:10).

Yes, my soul, find rest in God; my hope comes from him. Truly he is my Rock and my salvation; he is my fortress, I will not be shaken. - **(Psalm 62:5-6).**

Yes, my soul, find rest in God; my hope comes from him. Truly he is my rock and my salvation; he is my fortress, I will not be shaken. -b**(1 Peter 2:9).**

RIGHT ATTITUDE

It is important to have a positive and right attitude because that will determine how far you will go in life. "It is your attitude, more than your aptitude, that will determine your altitude" (Zig Ziglar). If you have the right attitude, it will lead to happiness, good outcomes, and success in life.

> "IT IS YOUR ATTITUDE, MORE THAN YOUR APTITUDE, THAT WILL DETERMINE YOUR ALTITUDE" (ZIG ZIGLAR).

A right attitude causes you to be a source of good energy to everyone around you. It is your attitude toward others that will determine how they will treat you.

We all have different views of life; hence, we need to respect other people's views.

In your relationships with one another, have the same mindset as Christ Jesus: Who, being in very nature God, did not consider equality with God something to be used to his own advantage; rather, he made himself nothing by taking the very nature of a servant, being made in human likeness. And being found in appearance as a man, he humbled himself by becoming obedient to death even death on a cross! Therefore God exalted him to the highest place and gave him the name that is above every name, that at the name of Jesus every knee should bow, in heaven and on earth and under the earth, and every tongue acknowledges that Jesus Christ is Lord, to the glory of God the Father.

- **(Philippians 2:5-11).**

Finally, brothers and sisters, whatever is true, whatever is noble, whatever is right, whatever is pure, whatever is lovely, whatever is admirable if anything is excellent or praiseworthy think about such things. - **(Philippians 4:8).**

Get rid of all bitterness, rage and anger, brawling and slander, along with every form of malice. Be kind and compassionate to one another, forgiving each other, just as in Christ God forgave you. - **(Ephesians 4:31-32).**

MENTAL GLORY - WISDOM

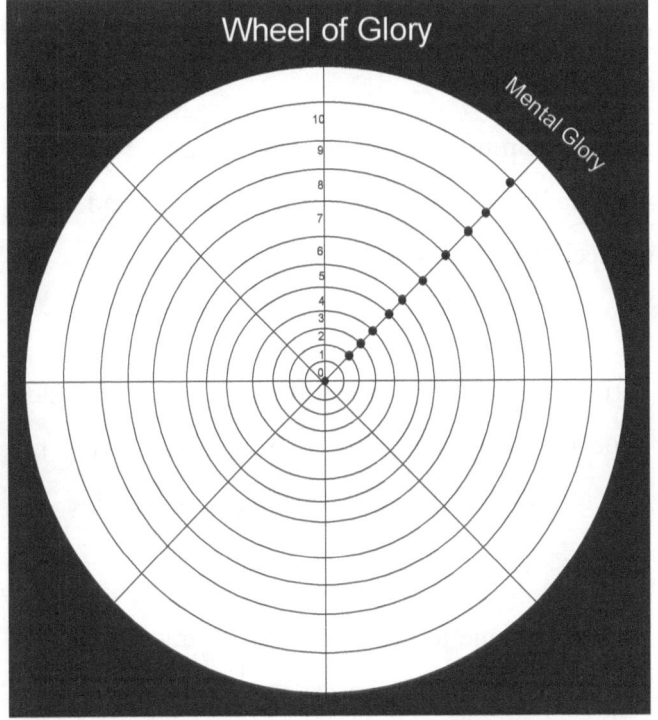

The diagram above is to help you see where you are on your journey.

Between 0 - 10, what score are you going to give yourself? What are the mental things you need to give attention to in your life? How are you planning to put them into action so you can accomplish them?

PRAYERS

Father, help me to discover who I am in You. Help me to know my self-worth in You, and daily appreciate all You have deposited in me.

Father, Help me to develop myself daily and add value to the lives of others around me. Show me how to set goals that are realistic and achievable.

Father, help me to break through all my limitations. Whatever is standing before me stopping me from reaching my goals in life, I receive grace and strength from You today to deal with them.

Father, help me to have the right attitude towards the people around me. My attitude will lead to my altitude in life. Help me to have a positive attitude that will lead to my success in life.

Father, Make me a homemaker. Give me the grace to manage my home and to be an entrepreneur by nature. Father, give me a sound mind.

Father, renew my mindset. Change every wrong mindset I have and please, help me to overcome.
In Jesus' name, I pray.

ACTION PLAN SHEET

1. SET GOALS YOU WANT TO ACHIEVE IN THESE AREAS OF YOUR LIFE.

_____
_____
_____
_____

2. PUT A PLAN INTO PLACE ON HOW TO ACHIEVE YOUR GOALS.

_____
_____
_____
_____

3. LOOK FOR AREAS THAT NEED IMPROVEMENT IN ORDER FOR YOU TO ACHIEVE THESE GOALS.

_____
_____
_____
_____

MENTAL GLORY - WISDOM

4. SCRIPTURES TO STAND ON.

_____
_____
_____
_____

Chapter Nine
EMOTIONAL GLORY

A glorious woman must have control over her emotions. This is absolutely important because emotions can directly affect our behaviours, which, in turn, affect the way we treat other people in our lives.

Taking care of our emotions is crucial; it is an important part of our overall health. People who are healthy emotionally have control over their thoughts and feelings; they

> PEOPLE WHO ARE HEALTHY EMOTIONALLY HAVE CONTROL OVER THEIR THOUGHTS FEELINGS AND BEHAVIOURS.

also have control over their behaviours.

Like a city whose walls are broken through is a person who lacks self-control. - **(Proverbs 25:28).**

In this chapter dealing with emotional glory, we will look at 5 different areas a glorious woman needs to have control over.

1. Anger
2. Self
3. Relationship
4. Conflict management
5. Forgiveness

1. ANGER CONTROL

The Bible encourages us not to let the sun go down on our anger. Anger can destroy a lot of things and lead to regret. You have every reason to express how you feel about any issue but allowing anger to take control of you is the danger you must

> ANGER CAN DESTROY A LOT OF THINGS AND LEAD TO REGRET.

try to avoid. If you have anger problems, you need to seek help. Don't be ashamed to do so because it will provide you with solutions. Always feed on the Word of God and ask God for the Holy Spirit's help to control your anger.

In your anger do not sin": Do not let the sun go down while you are still angry, and do not give the devil a foothold. Anyone who has been stealing must steal no longer, but must work, doing something useful with their own hands, that they may have something to share with those in need. Do not let any unwholesome talk come out of your mouths, but only what is helpful for building others up according to their needs, that it may benefit those who listen. And do not grieve the Holy Spirit of God, with whom you were sealed for the day of redemption. Get rid of all bitterness, rage and anger, brawling and slander, along with every form of malice **(Ephesians 4:26-31).**

It is better to dwell in a corner of the housetop than with a contentious (troublesome) woman in a wide (big) house **(Proverbs 21:9).**

It is better to dwell in the wilderness, than with a contentious and angry woman (**Proverbs 21:19**).

SEVEN WAYS TO CONTROL YOUR ANGER

1. Pray to God for the grace to overcome anger
2. Don't react immediately to any situation
3. Find someone you can trust and discuss the situation with that person
4. See past the moment and look at the bigger picture
5. Get it out of your mind
6. Forgive
7. Seek professional help for anger management.

2. SELF-CONTROL

Self-control is the ability to control yourself, especially when you are facing difficult or challenging situations. It is the ability to exercise restraint or control over one's feelings,

> SELF-CONTROL KEEPS YOU FROM DOING THE NEGATIVE THINGS YOUR FEELINGS WANT YOU TO DO.

emotions, and reactions. Self-control keeps you from doing the negative things your feelings want you to do.

But the fruit of the Spirit is love, joy, peace, forbearance, kindness, goodness, faithfulness, gentleness and self-control. Against such things there is no law. - **(Galatians 5:22-23).**

Better a patient person than a warrior, one with self-control than one who takes a city. - **(Proverbs 16:32).**

3. GOOD INTERPERSONAL RELATIONSHIP

A glorious woman must have good interpersonal relationships. She must relate well to her family members and the people around her. She must also relate to:

- In-laws
- Siblings
- Neighbours
- Co-workers
- Church members
- Unbelievers around her

4. CONFLICT MANAGEMENT

Conflict is unpleasant but sometimes inevitable in business, home, the workplace and among the family. We will have disagreements, differences of opinion, and conflicting perspectives on various issues. However, as a glorious woman, you must know how to manage conflicts. Many times, people do things to us that are not right, and we have every reason to tell them how we feel. However, the way we communicate is important.

> GOD OFTEN USES CONFLICT TO REFINE OUR CHARACTERS.

Conflict can even cause us to doubt God's goodness, His will for our lives or His love for us. In fact, God often uses conflict to refine our characters, draw us closer to Him, and, ultimately, to glorify Himself.

CONFLICTS ARE INEVITABLE

Woe to the world because of the things that cause people to stumble! Such things must come, but woe to the person through whom they come! - **(Matthew 18:1).**

I urge you, brothers and sisters, to watch out for those who cause divisions and put obstacles in your way that are contrary to the teaching you have learned. Keep away from them. - **(Romans 16:17).**

Give no offense to Jews or Greeks or the church of God - **(1 Corinthians 10:32).**

BIBLE VERSES THAT TEACH US HOW TO HANDLE CONFLICT

Do not repay anyone evil for evil. Be careful to do what is right in the eyes of everyone. If it is possible, as far as it depends on you, live at peace with everyone. Do not take revenge, my dear friends, but leave room for God's wrath, for it is written: "It is mine to avenge; I will repay," says the Lord. On the contrary: "If your enemy is hungry, feed him; if he is thirsty, give him something to drink. In doing this, you will heap burning coals on his head." Do not be overcome by evil, but overcome evil with good - **(Romans 12:17-21).**

Finally, all of you, be like-minded, be sympathetic, love one another, and be compassionate and humble. Do not repay evil with evil or insult with insult. On the contrary, repay evil with blessing, because to this you were called so that you may inherit a blessing. For, "Whoever would love life and see good days must keep their tongue from evil and their lips from deceitful speech. They must turn from evil and do good; they must seek peace and pursue it. - **(1 Peter 3:8-11).**

You have heard that it was said, 'Eye for eye, and tooth for tooth. But I tell you, do not resist an evil person. If anyone slaps you on the right cheek, turn to them the other cheek also. And if anyone wants to sue you and take your shirt, hand over your coat as well. If anyone forces you to go one mile, go with them two miles. Give to the one who asks you, and do not turn away from the one who wants to borrow from you. - **(Matthew 5:38-42).**

5. FORGIVENESS

According to *Oxford Dictionaries*, forgiveness is the process of forgiving. You stop feeling angry or resentful towards someone for an offence, flaw or mistake.

Forgiveness can be difficult because people will do or say things that offend us. Rather than holding grudges against them, the Bible teaches us to forgive them. The Bible also reveals how God wants us to forgive. This is a very sensitive area; many times, we tend to bottle up our anger, and we choose not to forgive, not to release whoever has offended us. God wants us to forgive because having an unforgiving heart leads to bitterness. A heart that is bitter is heavy, troubled, and cannot love as it ought to love. On the other hand, when we forgive others, we are set free from all the negative feelings that come when we don't forgive.

> GOD WANTS US TO FORGIVE BECAUSE HAVING AN UNFORGIVING HEART LEADS TO BITTERNESS.

Then Peter came to Jesus and asked, "Lord, how many times shall I forgive my brother or sister who sins against me? Up to seven times?" Jesus answered, "I tell you, not seven times, but seventy-seven times. - **(Matthew 18:21-22).**

Bear with each other and forgive one another if any of you has a grievance against someone. Forgive as the Lord forgave you. - **(Colossians 3:13).**

SIX SUPER THINGS THAT HAPPEN WHEN WE FORGIVE OTHERS.

1. Forgiveness frees us from hurt, pain, resentment, and anger.

2. Forgiveness stops us from seeking revenge.

3. Forgiveness lets us move on.

4. Forgiveness brings us back to good physical and mental health.

5. Forgiveness lets you see all the positive qualities of the person who hurt you.

6. Forgiveness gives you a chance at a long-lasting, healthy relationship.

We have to forgive to let go of past pain. We have to heal. No matter what has happened in the past, our desire is to move on and see how to make things better.

SEVEN WAYS TO LET GO OF PAST HURTS

1. Decide to let it go
2. Stop blaming others
3. Stop blaming yourself
4. Don't focus on the past
5. Focus on the present
6. Forgive others
7. Forgive yourself

THE GLORIOUS WOMAN

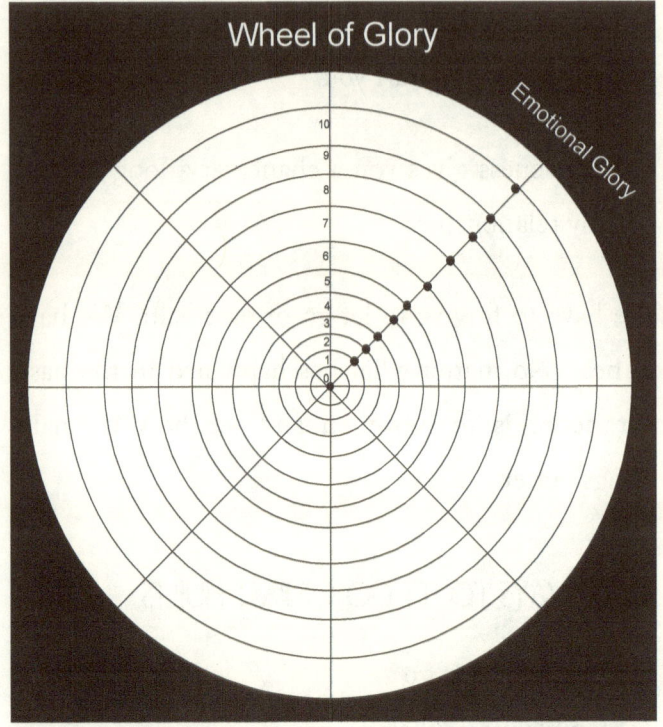

The diagram above is to help you see where you are on your journey.

Between 0 – 10, what score are you going to give yourself as related to attributes of Emotional Glory? What specific emotional attributes do you need to give attention to in your life? What are the required action steps that you need to take to be able to manifest full Emotional Glory in your life?

Prayers

Father, help me to control my emotions; they affect the way I behave towards others. Help me to control my anger and to have self-control in all I do. Help me to have good relationships with everybody around me.

Fether, Give me the grace to relate well with others. Help me to manage conflicts properly and to forgive others.

Father, help me to let go of the pains of the past. Whatever I have held onto in my life, give me the strength to let it go. Heal me completely from any pain of the past.

Father, unforgiveness is a huge monster that destroys completely. I don't want it to destroy me. Help me not to seek revenge. Heal me completely from all my pains so that I can let go.

Father, help me to have self-control over my emotions and my anger. I don't want to live a life of regret. Give me the grace to deal with my emotions. I believe I can do all things through Christ who strengthens me.

In Jesus' name, I pray.

THE GLORIOUS WOMAN

ACTION PLAN SHEET

1. SET GOALS YOU WANT TO ACHIEVE IN THESE AREAS OF YOUR LIFE.

_____
_____
_____
_____

2. PUT A PLAN INTO PLACE ON HOW TO ACHIEVE YOUR GOALS.

_____
_____
_____
_____

3. LOOK FOR AREAS THAT NEED IMPROVEMENT IN ORDER FOR YOU TO ACHIEVE THESE GOALS.

_____
_____
_____
_____

4. SCRIPTURES TO STAND ON.

_____
_____
_____
_____

Chapter Ten

PHYSICAL GLORY

GOOD PHYSICAL APPEARANCE

We have to appreciate the beauty God has given us because it reveals the glory of God's creative abilities. Our physical appearance is very important to God who crafted each of us.

A glorious woman must keep a good physical appearance before and after marriage.

She should not neglect herself at any time and should always do her best to be attractive to her husband and those around her. Her look is important to God. She must keep her hair, nails, and face tidy at all times.

How beautiful you are, my darling! Oh, how beaut-iful! Your eyes are doves. - **(Songs of Solomon 1:15).**

CLEANLINESS

As glorious women, we must keep our environments clean. We must keep our living rooms, kitchens, toilets, bathrooms, garages, pantries, and bedrooms clean. These are our homes. Cleanliness is utmost; it is not negotiable. The kitchen sink must be clean. If we are too busy, we can get a cleaner to do the tidying and laundry for us.

One day Ruth's mother-in-law Naomi said to her, "My daughter, I must find a home for you, where you will be well provided for. Now Boaz, with whose women you have worked, is a relative of ours. Tonight he will be winnowing barley on the threshing floor. Wash, put on perfume, and get dressed in your best clothes. Then go down to the

threshing floor, but don't let him know you are there until he has finished eating and drinking.
- **(Ruth 3:1-3, NKJV).**

KEEPING YOUR BODY IN GOOD SHAPE

The Bible says our bodies are God's temple. As a glorious woman, you must mind what you eat. Eating healthy food is necessary because it helps you to keep in shape. Men love their women to be smart and look good. You can do daily exercises to help you burn calories or join the gym so you can have the support of an instructor.

Do you not know that your bodies are temples of the Holy Spirit, who is in you, whom you have received from God? You are not your own; you were bought at a price. Therefore honor God with your bodies. **(1 Corinthians 6:19-20).**

Have nothing to do with godless myths and old wives' tales; rather, train yourself to be godly. For physical training is of some value, but godliness has

value for all things, holding promise for both the present life and the life to come. This is a trustworthy saying that deserves full acceptance.
- **(1 Timothy 4:7-9).**

WEIGHT MANAGEMENT

Managing your weight means focusing on a healthy lifestyle. You have to eat healthy foods, and do regular exercise. Keeping your body weight under control is very important. We tend to lose the ability to do a lot of things when we are overweight. This can really be frustrating. Being overweight or obese creates several issues for us as women. It leads to an increase in blood pressure. High blood pressure is the main cause of strokes. Excess weight also increases your chances of developing other problems linked to strokes including high cholesterol, high blood sugar, and heart disease. You have to visit a good dietician to help you with your menu plan.

> MANAGING YOUR WEIGHT MEANS FOCUSING ON A HEALTHY LIFESTYLE.

A cheerful heart is good medicine, but a crushed spirit dries up the bones. - **(Proverbs 17:22, TLB).**

Trouble and distress have come upon me, but your commands give me delight. - **(Psalm 119:143).**

GOOD CLOTHING

Are my clothing choices bringing glory to God? That is a great question every glorious woman must ask herself. Modesty is not anti-fashion; it is a way of adorning God. We must have this at the back of our minds when we choose the clothes we buy as glorious women.

> MODESTY IS NOT ANTI-FASHION; IT IS A WAY OF ADORNING GOD WITH YOUR BODY.

Good colour combinations are essential. A glorious woman must know how to combine her clothes well. She must be comfortable in well-fitted clothing and stylish. The material should be of good quality. You don't have to buy expensive clothes to look good.

Do you not know that your bodies are temples of the Holy Spirit, who is in you, whom you have received from God? You are not your own; you were bought at a price. Therefore honour God with your bodies. - **(1 Corinthians 6:19-20)**

Therefore, I urge you, brothers and sisters, in view of God's mercy, to offer your bodies as a living sacrifice, holy and pleasing to God—this is your true and proper worship. – **(Romans 12:1).**

DRESS YOURSELF WITH STRENGTH AND DIGNITY, NOT SEDUCTIVE.

We should dress in a way that shows reverence and respect to God. Moreover, we must also show dignity and respect for ourselves, as well as others around us. Being modest in appearance is very important. The Bible tells us about a woman who dresses based on her heart. For example, if a woman likes to dress sensually, her heart is evil as well. This scripture from Proverbs proves that a woman does not need to dress in a sexy way for a man to like her.

If a woman is clothed with strength and dignity, she will be confident enough to say, "I am God's wonderful and beautiful creation."

She is clothed with strength and dignity; she can laugh at the days to come. - **(Proverbs 31:25).**

I also want the women to dress modestly, with decency and propriety, adorning themselves, not with elaborate hairstyles or gold or pearls or expensive clothes, but with good deeds, appropriate for women who profess to worship God. - **(1Timothy 2: 9-10).**

PERSONAL HYGIENE

Women's hygiene is important for many reasons. We sweat, menstruate, and have vaginal discharges. We have to prevent body odours and maintain good hygiene as a priority. To do so, we should pay special attention to bathing, using deodorants, and wearing clean clothes, so we can always smell fresh and good.

THE GLORIOUS WOMAN

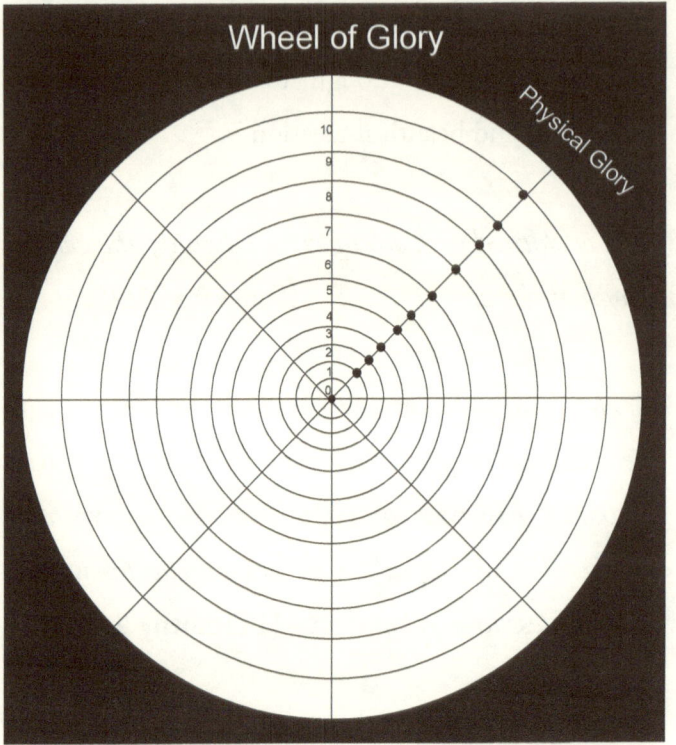

The diagram above is to help you see where you are on your journey.

Between 0 – 10, what score are you going to give yourself as related to attributes of Physical Glory? What specific physical attributes do you need to give attention to in your life? What are the required action steps that you need to take to be able to manifest full Physical Glory in your life?

PRAYERS

Father, Help me to always stay beautiful and attractive. Help me to live a healthy lifestyle. Give me the grace to work on me and not neglect myself.

Father, Help me to be a good role model by the way I dress, as well as decent and godly in the things I wear. I don't want others to fall because of my attire. My body is to bring glory to You.

Father, Help me to keep my home clean and give me the wisdom to prioritise and do my daily tasks. Father, I pray that daily You will help me to get better with the work I do in my house.

Father, help me to overcome my challenges, all my frustrations, and to deal with whatever is bothering me that is affecting the way I look and dress. Give me strength.

Father, My body belongs to You; it is the dwelling place of Your Spirit. Father, give me the grace to accept and celebrate all the changes in my body. Help me to control what I eat and drink.

In Jesus' name, I pray.

ACTION PLAN SHEET

1. SET GOALS YOU WANT TO ACHIEVE IN THESE AREAS OF YOUR LIFE.

_____
_____
_____
_____

2. PUT A PLAN INTO PLACE ON HOW TO ACHIEVE YOUR GOALS.

_____
_____
_____
_____

3. LOOK FOR AREAS THAT NEED IMPROVEMENT IN ORDER FOR YOU TO ACHIEVE THESE GOALS.

_____
_____
_____
_____

THE GLORIOUS WOMAN

4. SCRIPTURES TO STAND ON.

_____

_____

_____

_____

Chapter Eleven

CONFESSION OF THE GLORIOUS WOMAN

- I confess I am coming out of shame to honour and praise
- I confess I am coming out of regret to joy
- I confess I am coming out of rejection to acceptance

- I confess I am coming out of pain to comfort
- I confess I am coming out of sickness to health
- I confess I am coming out of oppression to freedom
- I confess I am coming out of embarrassment to dignity
- I confess I am coming out of debt to riches
- I confess I am coming out of lack to superabundance
- I confess I am coming out of hopelessness to expectation
- I confess I am coming out of ignorance to wisdom and knowledge
- I confess I am coming out of neglect to focus
- I confess I am coming out of opposition to acceptance
- I confess I am coming out of financial hardship to financial recovery
- I confess I am born to reign
- I confess I am born to dominate

PHYSICAL GLORY

- I confess I am born to fulfil purpose
- I confess I am born to occupy.
- I confess I am born to rest
- I confess I am born to be fruitful
- I confess I am born to have a good life
- I confess I am born to inherit honour
- I confess I am born to be favoured
- I confess I am born to overcome
- I confess I am born to be celebrated
- I confess I am born to gain wisdom
- I confess I am born to gain insight
- I confess I am born to gain foresight
- I confess I am born to gain revelation
- I confess I am born to multiply
- I confess I am born to be blessed and also be a blessing.
- I confess I am born to inherit the land

Chapter Twelve

PRAYER OF TRANSFORMATION FOR THE GLORIOUS WOMAN

Lord Jesus, transform me; renew my mind and my understanding of myself. I pray I will not judge myself by the standards of this world. Keep me focused on who I am in You. Lord Jesus, renew my thinking.

Lord Jesus, Your Word reveals my identity. I am wonderfully and fearfully made; help me to remove any contrary opinion about myself. Take away every negative thought I have about myself. Help me to see the treasure in me and to appreciate the fact that I am a product of the almighty God. Help me to see the excellent things about me rather than pulling myself down.

Lord Jesus, help me to carry myself with grace. Let me see every change in me as a divine plan from You, rather than hating and complaining about myself. In You I live; in You I move; in You I have my being. My beauty is rooted in You. I refuse to use the language of this world on myself.

Lord Jesus, teach me to be grateful for every stage in my life that I have gone through. Help me to always remember that You love and care for me.

Lord Jesus, don't let me focus my attention on the things that are not eternal. Help me not to worry about my physical looks. There is much pressure in the world, but You can show me how to express myself in ways that please You. Show me that the fashion standards of the world are not set for me. I have not built my values, beauty, boldness, and confidence in their standards.

Lord Jesus, I affirm that I am wonderfully and beautifully created. I am a carrier of Your image, and You have called me good. I refuse to be ashamed of me. I refuse to hate myself. I refuse to accept the decision of the world about my beauty. In Jesus' name, I pray.

Lord Jesus, help me to display boldness, confidence, good self-esteem, and self-acceptance. There is no law against these great virtues. The Bible says, "Finally, brethren, whatsoever things are true, whatsoever things are honest, whatsoever things are just, whatsoever things are pure, whatsoever things are lovely, whatsoever things are of good report; if there be any virtue, and if there be any praise, think on these things" (Philippians 4:8). Lord Jesus, help me to focus on the things that are true and good as

Your Word says. Teach me to embrace the truth and not compromise that I may accept and do what You love.

Lord Jesus, help me to keep fashion in the right perspective and to appreciate my inner beauty, which is most valuable to You. Give me the grace to shine the light that is in me. Let people see the light and come to You. As I stay in Your presence Lord Jesus, let me glow.

Lord Jesus, those who look up to You are always radiant. Help me to continually stay in this truth and trust You enough. Their faces are never covered with shame. Remove any shame I have in my appearance because You are looking at the heart.

Lord Jesus, where others are pulling me down and talking about my beauty, let me find strength in knowing You are looking at my heart. You want me to please You, and this is the beauty I have.

Lord Jesus, I affirm that I am created to do good works; therefore, good works alone I will do. The Devil has come to steal, kill, and destroy, but You have come to give life in abundance. Help me to find life in every good work I am created to do.

HOW TO BE SAVED

If you haven't known God personally, here are four principles that will help guide you into a relationship with him:

1. GOD LOVES YOU AND CREATED YOU TO KNOW HIM PERSONALLY.

The most well-known verse in the Bible says, *"God so loved the world, that he gave his only Son, that whoever believes in him should not perish but have eternal life"* - **(John 3:16, ESV).**

You see, this life is not the end of us. This life is preparation for eternity. We have the freedom to decide where we want to spend eternity: with God or apart from God.

God thinks you're so valuable that he wants to spend eternity with you! The Bible says, *"Now this is eternal life: that they may know you, the only true God, and Jesus Christ, whom you have sent"* - **(John 17:3)**.

He planned the universe and orchestrated history, including the details of our lives, so that we could become his friends.

So, what prevents us from knowing God personally?

2. MAN IS SINFUL AND SEPARATED FROM GOD, SO WE CANNOT KNOW HIM PERSONALLY OR EXPERIENCE HIS LOVE BECAUSE OF OUR SIN.

The Bible says, *"All have sinned and fall short of the glory of God"* - **(Romans 3:23)**.

Visualize God in heaven and man on earth, with a great gulf separating the two. Man is continually trying to reach God and establish a personal relationship with him through his own efforts, such as a good life, philosophy, or religion—but he inevitably fails.

The Bible says, "*The wages of sin is death* [separation from God]" **(Romans 6:23)**. The third principle explains the only way to bridge this separation.

3. JESUS CHRIST IS GOD'S ONLY PROVISION FOR MAN'S SIN. THROUGH HIM ALONE CAN WE KNOW GOD PERSONALLY AND EXPERIENCE GOD'S LOVE.

JESUS DIED IN OUR PLACE.

"God demonstrates his own love for us in this: While we were still sinners, Christ died for us"
- **(Romans 5:8 NIV).**

HE ROSE FROM THE DEAD.

"Christ died for our sins, just as the Scriptures said. He was buried, and he was raised from the dead on the third day, just as the Scriptures said. He was seen by Peter and then by the Twelve. After that,

he was seen by more than 500 of his followers at one time . . ."- **(1 Corinthians 15:3-6, NLT).**

HE IS THE ONLY WAY TO GOD.

"Jesus said to him, 'I am the way, and the truth, and the life; no one comes to the Father, but through Me'"- **(John 14:6 NASB).**

Visualize now that God has bridged the gulf that separates us from him by sending his Son, Jesus Christ, to die on the cross in our place to pay the penalty for our sins. Yet it's not enough just to know these truths . . .

4. WE MUST INDIVIDUALLY RECEIVE JESUS CHRIST AS SAVIOR AND LORD; THEN WE CAN KNOW GOD PERSONALLY AND EXPERIENCE HIS LOVE.

WE MUST RECEIVE CHRIST.

"As many as received him, to them he gave the right to become children of God, even to those who believe in his name"- **(John 1:12 NASB).**

WE RECEIVE CHRIST THROUGH FAITH.

"It is by grace you have been saved, through faith- and this not from yourselves, it is the gift of God- not by works, so that no one can boast" **- (Ephesians 2:8–9 NIV).**

WHEN WE RECEIVE CHRIST, WE EXPERIENCE A NEW BIRTH.

The Bible tells of how a man named Nicodemus experienced a new birth through Christ:

There was a man named Nicodemus, a Jewish religious leader who was a Pharisee. After dark one evening, he came to speak with Jesus. "Rabbi," he said, "we all know that God has sent you to teach us. Your miraculous signs are evidence that God is with you."

Jesus replied, "I tell you the truth, unless you are born again, you cannot see the Kingdom of God." "What do you mean?" exclaimed Nicodemus. "How can an old man go back into his mother's womb and be born again?"

Jesus replied, "I assure you, no one can enter the Kingdom of God without being born of water and the Spirit. Humans can reproduce only human life, but the Holy Spirit gives birth to spiritual life. So don't be surprised when I say, You must be born again. The wind blows wherever it wants. Just as you can hear the wind but can't tell where it comes from or where it is going, so you can't explain how people are born of the Spirit."
- *(John 3:1-8, NLT)*

WE RECEIVE CHRIST BY PERSONAL INVITATION

Jesus Christ says, "Behold, I stand at the door and knock; if anyone hears my voice and opens the door, I will come in to him and dine with him, and he with me." - **(Revelation 3:20, NASB)**

Receiving Christ involves turning to God from self and trusting Christ to come into our lives to forgive us of our sins and to make us what he wants us to be. Just to agree intellectually that Jesus Christ is the Son of God and that he died on the cross for our sins is not enough. Nor is it enough to have an emotional experience. We receive Jesus Christ by faith, as an act of our free will.

HOW YOU CAN RECEIVE CHRIST RIGHT NOW BY FAITH THROUGH PRAYER

Prayer is just talking with God. He knows your heart, so don't worry about getting your words just right. Here is a suggested prayer to guide you:

Lord Jesus, I want to know you personally. Thank you for dying on the cross for my sins.

I open the door of my life and receive you as my Saviour and Lord.

Thank you for forgiving me of my sins and giving me eternal life.

Take control of my life. Make me the kind of person You want me to be.

Does this prayer express the desire of your heart? If it does, pray this prayer right now, and Christ will come into your life as promised.

Did you pray to receive Christ just now? If so, Congratulations! Luke 15:7 says that when one sinner accepts Jesus Christ as his or her Saviour the angels rejoice. So there's a party going on in heaven right now over your decision! Remember this date as your "second birthday," the day you were born into a new life in Christ! You have God's Word that he answered your prayer.

The Bible promises eternal life to all who receive Christ: *"God has given us eternal life, and this life is in his Son. He who has the Son has the life; he who does not have the Son of God does not have the life. I write these things to you who believe in the name of the Son of God so that you may know that you have eternal life"* - **(1 John 5:11–13 NIV)**.

Thank God often that Christ is in your life and that he will never leave you. - **(Hebrews 13:5).**

You can know on the basis of his promise that Christ lives in you and that you have eternal life from the very moment you invited Him in.

www.ingramcontent.com/pod-product-compliance
Lightning Source LLC
Chambersburg PA
CBHW032039290426
44110CB00012B/870